INVESTING THE

Templeton Way

INVESTING THE
Templeton Way

*The Market-Beating
Strategies of
Value Investing's
Legendary
Bargain Hunter*

LAUREN C. TEMPLETON | **SCOTT PHILLIPS**

New York   Chicago   San Francisco   Lisbon   London   Madrid
Mexico City   Milan   New Delhi   San Juan   Seoul
Singapore   Sydney   Toronto

The McGraw·Hill Companies

1 2 3 4 5 6 7 8 9 0 DOC/DOC 0 9 8

ISBN: 978-1-265-62146-9
MHID: 1-26-562146-2

This publication is designed to provide accurate and authoritative information in regard to the subject matter covered. It is sold with the understanding that the publisher is not engaged in rendering legal, accounting, or other professional service. If legal advice or other expert assistance is required, the services of a competent professional person should be sought.
> —From a Declaration of Principles Jointly Adopted by a Committee of the American Bar Association and a Committee of Publishers and Associations

McGraw-Hill books are available at special quantity discounts to use as premiums and sales promotions, or for use in corporate training programs. To contact a representative, please visit the Contact Us pages at www.mhprofessional.com.

For our mentors, Sir John Marks Templeton and
Handly Cotton Templeton

And in loving memory of Harvey Maxwell Templeton, Junior,
and David Phillips

CONTENTS

FOREWORD

I am approaching my ninety-fifth birthday and believe that there has never been a better time to be alive. We should be deeply grateful to have been born in this age of unbelievable prosperity. At my age, I devote almost all my efforts and resources to the Templeton Foundations, which focus on building spiritual wealth for humanity worldwide.

Investors to this day write to me for investing advice or to express concerns about the global economy. Throughout history, people have focused too little on the opportunities that problems present in investing and in life in general. In my lifetime, we have been blessed by so many remarkable achievements. The twenty-first century offers great hope and glorious promise, perhaps a new golden age of opportunity.

Investing the Templeton Way provides a brief history of my investing career. My great-niece Lauren Templeton and her husband, Scott Phillips, describe the investing mentality of a bargain hunter. There are many investing methods available, but I have had the most success when purchasing stocks priced far too low in relation to their intrinsic worth. Throughout my investment career, I have searched the world for the best bargain stocks available. Research shows that a stock portfolio with investments around the world is likely to yield, in the long run, a higher return at a lower level of volatility than will a simple, diversified single-nation portfolio. Diversification should be the cornerstone of any investment program.

One principle that I have used throughout my career is to invest at the point of maximum pessimism. That is, the time to be most optimistic is at the point of maximum pessimism. *Investing the Templeton Way* describes methods I have used throughout my career to identify points of maximum pessimism in a stock, an industry, or a country.

In almost every activity in life people try to go where the outlook is best. You look for a job in an industry with a good future or build a factory in an area where the prospects are best. However, my contention is that if you are selecting publicly traded investments, you have to do the opposite. You are trying to buy a share at the lowest possible price in relation to what a corporation is worth. There is only one reason a stock is being offered at a bargain price: because other people are selling. There is no other reason. To get a bargain price, you have to look where the public is most frightened and pessimistic. Whenever you purchase a large amount of future earning power for a low price, you have made a good investment. The only way to accomplish this is to buy when others are selling. Investors often struggle with this concept; it is not easy to act contrary to popular opinion. I have relied on the following motto throughout my investment career:

> To buy when others are despondently selling and to sell when others are avidly buying requires the greatest of fortitude and pays the greatest ultimate reward.

It is my hope that after reading this book investors will have the skills and confidence required to buy low and sell high. Often this means avoiding what is popular. You may find it helpful to remember this advice:

> Bull markets are born on pessimism, grow on skepticism, mature on optimism, and die on euphoria. The time of maximum pessimism is the best time to buy, and the time of maximum optimism is the best time to sell.

John M. Templeton
September 2007

Chapter | 1

THE BIRTH OF A
BARGAIN HUNTER

*At the beginning of sophomore year [1931] my father told me with
regret that he could not contribute even one dollar more to my
education. At first this seemed like a tragedy, but now, looking back, it
was the best thing that could have happened.*

—Sir John Templeton

A large part of who we are is established in our early years. In the case of my great-uncle Sir John Templeton (Uncle John), it will become readily apparent that a great deal of his approach to life, investing, and philanthropy is rooted in his childhood. Growing up in the small town of Winchester, Tennessee, Uncle John was handed a set of values by his parents, Harvey and Vella. Those values would guide him regardless of the circumstances or situation he found himself in at any time. Primarily, his earliest virtues were thrift, an industrious nature, curiosity, and quiet self-assuredness. If I had to characterize his personality in one phrase, it would be "eternally optimistic." What we will come to find out is that those virtues were the result of a unique laissez-faire style of parenting coupled with the profound experiences of his late teens and early adult years, which coincided with the Great Depression. Most important, we will explore how those virtues and collective experiences built the foundation for a man who would become one of the world's most successful investors.

Uncle John is often referred to as a value investor when it comes to classifying his investment style. The term *value investor* brings up connotations of the seminal investor Benjamin Graham, who authored the book *Security Analysis*. Graham is credited for mentoring and shaping the investing style of another world-famous investor, Warren Buffett. In short, there is no question that Uncle John applied the early methods of Graham in his own investment approach, but he eventually expounded on those well-known and often prescribed methods. Setting aside the teachings of Benjamin Graham for now, let us simplify the definition of a value investor. We consider a value investor to be an individual who attempts to pay less than what he or she believes is the true value of a specific asset or object. At the core of this definition is a simple but critical assumption: The price of an asset or object can differ from its true value or worth.

In light of the long line of value investors who have followed Benjamin Graham's teachings, it probably is assumed that Uncle John read *Security Analysis*, applied its methods, and the rest was history. However, this is not entirely the case. By the time Uncle John picked up a copy of *Security Analysis*, as a young man entering the investment counsel business in the 1930s, his birth as a value investor had already occurred much earlier.

When he was a child, Uncle John's father (and my great-grandfather), Harvey Sr., was a lawyer in Winchester. Harvey's office was on the town square, and his window overlooked the county courthouse.

During the middle to late 1920s and extending into the Depression, Harvey often explored methods of accumulating wealth outside his law practice. Some of those methods included running a cotton gin, selling insurance, renting out dwellings, and buying land such as farms. Interestingly, it was the practice of buying up farms that provided Uncle John, then a young boy, with his first lesson in value investing. Because the income generated from farming in the 1920s often was limited—about $200 per year on average, according to Uncle John—those business ventures often led to failure and, unfortunately, foreclosure. Generally, when farms were foreclosed on, they would be sold at auction on the town square of Winchester and awarded to the highest bidder.

As the farms came up for auction on the town square, Harvey Sr. had a keen vantage point on the auction and its progress from his second-floor office window. When the auctions failed to produce a bidder, Harvey Sr. would leave his office and walk downstairs to the square and bid on the properties. Usually, in those instances Harvey Sr. was able to buy farms for just a few cents on the dollar, and by the mid-1920s he had accumulated six properties. Uncle John's observation of this practice as a young boy probably represents the very first seed of his most famous investing approach, which he termed buying at the point of "maximum pessimism" or "the principle of maximum pessimism." As you might have guessed, the practice of buying properties at such low prices, much lower than their actual *worth*, eventually created greater wealth as Uncle John's older brother, Harvey Jr. (my grandfather), decades later sold the properties to commercial and residential developers.

The fact that those farms could not attract any other buyers may seem mind-boggling in hindsight. However, as we will discover through our chronicles of Uncle John's great investments over his multidecade career as a money manager, those very circumstances are repeated over and over in the world's stock markets. The philosophy that Uncle John used as an investor is not much different from the way his father bought farms for a fraction of what they were worth on the steps of a courthouse when there were no other bidders. Most of us can see that in an auction, if you are the only bidder, you can get a favorable price, perhaps even a steal. Taking this relationship a step further, it has always been one of the great ironies of the stock market that when stocks drop in price, or "go on sale," they attract fewer buyers. Conversely, when stocks become more expensive, they attract increasing numbers of buyers because of their popularity. Uncle John's early childhood observation that a valuable farm could be purchased for cents on the dollar simply because there were no other buyers around—not because the farms were worthless—formed a deep impression that remained with him throughout his life.

Sometimes a valuable lesson comes from observing and then applying the successful actions of another person. However, even wiser people observe painful events and adopt them as experience without personally repeating them. Simply put, the wise person learns from his or her own mistakes, but the wiser person learns from the mistakes of others. Uncle John's next formative lesson also came from his father, but in this case it was due to a reversal of good fortune.

As we mentioned earlier, Uncle John's father was involved in many business ventures. As the owner and operator of a cotton gin and bonded cotton warehouses, Harvey Sr. owned one of only three operations in Franklin County, Tennessee, and it was relatively productive in its day. One characteristic of my great-grandfather that we have not discussed is that most of those who knew him in my family describe him as a "hit it rich" kind of guy, always looking for the next opportunity to hit pay dirt. One of his attempts at that goal was to make large investments in cotton futures on the New York and New Orleans cotton exchanges. Uncle John and my grandfather always told the tale of the day their father walked into the house and said, "Boys, we've made it rich, we just made more money than you can imagine in the cotton futures market, you will never have to work another day in your lives, neither will your children or grandchildren. . . ." The boys were elated, but only a few days later Harvey Sr. walked into the house, looked at his children, and said, "Boys, we've lost it all; we're ruined."

Witnessing this emotional, if not breathless, journey from wealth to despair was clearly Uncle John's first lesson in risk management and the ethereal nature of paper wealth created by financial markets. This example of boom and bust success rates would typify my great-grandfather's business life. In sum, his impulsive business dealings and lack of savings often left him financially unstable. Later in his life he reached the point of borrowing from Uncle John and my grandfather to support those habits. Undoubtedly, witnessing those events during their young lives pushed Uncle John and my grandfather toward adopting a deep respect for thrift. Both children grew into men who took thrift to an "artistic" level defined by creative ways to save money. Both found that comfort and security always accompany the practice of saving.

Uncle John always reminds us that when he and his first wife moved to New York shortly after their marriage, to begin his investment career they made it a rule to save *half* of their income. For every dollar that came in, 50 cents was set aside and invested. Uncle John said that to enable this high level of savings he and his wife, Judith, would turn the task into a game of sorts. When Uncle John and Judith moved into their first unfurnished apartment in New York, they scoured the newspapers in search of furniture auctions and estate sales. By the time they were finished, they had furnished their five-room apartment for $25 (for curious readers, this equates to approximately $351 in 2006 dollars). They even enlisted friends in the challenge of spotting bargains, including good blue-plate specials around the city. The goal in this case was a meal for $0.50 ($7.03 in 2006 dollars).

Uncle John and his wife turned themselves into consummate bargain hunters. Their bargain hunting was more about spotting a great deal than it was about buying cheap stuff. One of Uncle John's favorite deals was paying $5 for a $200 sofa bed. Since the economy was still working its way out of the Depression, they were able to take advantage of personal bankruptcies and any auctions that attracted few bidders. A few years later, Uncle John and Judith moved into a house in Englewood, New Jersey, after the birth of their first child, Jack. They were able to purchase a home for $5,000 in cash, which they sold five years later for $17,000. In case you were wondering, that is a compounded return of nearly 28 percent over five years. Not bad, considering that we have not yet started to discuss his stock investments. The underlying principle that Uncle John always used in these instances was to pay for everything in cash so that they "would always be *receivers* and not *payers* of interest." This was important to him throughout his life. He never had a mortgage, never borrowed to buy a car, and always had enough savings to make it through a rough patch.

As we are beginning to see in the case of my great-uncle, bargain hunting does not have to be relegated to investments alone. Instead, it is a pervasive life philosophy that endures in Uncle John to this day. Searching for the best possible deal available is a mindset without bounds. It is in fact a lifestyle. Seeing the lengths to which Uncle John and Judith went to track down bargains is important because it is wholly analogous to the same intensive search process that Uncle John employed in searching for bargain stocks on a worldwide basis. In a sense, when Uncle John was poring over Value Line stock reports, company filings, and other materials in search of a cheap stock, this practice was an extension of an innate desire to buy something selling for less than what he supposed was its true worth. Whether it is furniture, a house, a meal, a stock, or a bond, it doesn't matter: Look for a bargain.

Another consideration is that by looking at his everyday purchases, we can get a better sense of what qualifies as a bargain to Uncle John. His idea of a bargain is a bit more extreme than that of the average person. To provide some insight into an actual quantification of what Uncle John would consider a good bargain, he often remarks that an asset selling at an 80 percent discount to what he believes to be its value represents such a find. In other words, an asset priced at 20 percent of its value—stated another way, selling for 20 cents on the dollar—represents a good bargain. It can be difficult locating bargains of this magnitude, but finding discounts this large is a worthy goal nonetheless.

Of course, it may seem curious that Uncle John took his daily practice of thrift and bargain hunting to such extremes. There was a good reason. This was not just a doctrinaire principle at work; it was a deliberate and focused attempt to save the money he needed to start his own investment counsel practice. Uncle John finally did reach that goal with the purchase of an investment counsel business run by an elderly man named George Towne. The business Uncle John bought had eight clients, and he paid $5,000 for the business, which he renamed Towne, Templeton and Dobbrow. A few years later his firm merged with Vance, Chapin and Company, and the name was changed to Templeton, Dobbrow, and Vance. During those early years of running his own firm, Uncle John relied on his savings to make it through the lean beginnings of running a small business; he often could not pay himself a salary.

It is very interesting to consider how Uncle John's early savings eventually enabled him to help hundreds of thousands of investors save and create wealth and security as his business career evolved into managing the Templeton Funds. It is important to note that this is not a trivial observation or coincidence. Instead, it was a driving force behind my great-uncle's immense success as an investor. Because Uncle John valued thrift so highly, he deemed it a virtue. In keeping with that belief system, he saw his job as helping others and bestowing the same benefits of wealth and security on those who saved. Uncle John did not aim for high returns in his funds only for the sake of high returns. He truly believed that his success as a fund manager was measured by the ability to enable his clients to send their children or grandchildren to college or plan for retirement. He took that responsibility very seriously.

Often in the world of business you will find that the most successful practitioners are driven to heights by a noble purpose. Although some successful businesspeople are driven by money, many are successful because of altruistic intentions. Although it often is misunderstood, Sam Walton's vision at Wal-Mart was to lower the cost of goods for Americans. He reasoned that this would put more discretionary money in their pockets and thus improve their lives. Henry Ford wanted to bring an automobile to the masses rather than sell to the wealthy alone like all the other carmakers at that time. Rose Blumkin, the original proprietor of Nebraska Furniture Mart (probably the most successful furniture store to date, now owned by Berkshire Hathaway), always told people that her objective was to make nice furniture affordable to improve the lives of her customers. This concept of "doing well by doing good" was popularized by Benjamin Franklin, and it has been a winning recipe for business success ever since.

It is no wonder, then, that Uncle John's early love affair with thrift and saving guided him to share his gift for compounding his investors' money in the best bargain stocks he could discover. Uncle John's practice of thrift, his talent for bargain hunting, and his fascination with the compounding of interest was the exact formula necessary to make good on the advice of his mother, Vella: "Find a need and fill it." The need he identified was improving people's lives by helping them create wealth, and his ability to fill that need was honed over the many years that led up to the launching of his own practice. By the time Uncle John began his own practice, he had determined his contribution to his fellow men and women and was executing that strategy during every waking moment.

Up until this point we have discussed the influence of Uncle John's father on his investment philosophy and belief system, but that does not mean that his mother was not influential. In fact, my great-grandmother was incredibly influential on Uncle John as she impressed upon him many of her Presbyterian and Unity School virtues, including the absolute importance of hard work and service to others. The importance of service to others is one of her most lasting influences on Uncle John, and it is easy to see that in his words: "Do something where you're performing a real service for people. It'll be a success. I like investment counseling. And I like helping others. It gives you pleasure you can't get spending thousands of dollars."

Those already familiar with Uncle John may have recognized his strong embrace of freedom of enterprise and free will. Those ideals came directly from his mother, Vella, who was in her time the freest of spirits and an enterpriser to match. For evidence, consider that by the 1920s, when Uncle John and my grandfather were young boys, she had traveled alone to Texas from Winchester to work as a tutor on the million-acre Kenedy Ranch. Vella was also exceptional in that she was high school– and college-educated in rural Tennessee in the early 1900s. Although these endeavors are impressive for that time, it is even more remarkable that she raised money for and continuously funded a Christian missionary named Gam Sin Qua in China.

In the eyes of the young John Templeton, there were no cultural or geographical boundaries. This perspective came directly from Vella. There was no acknowledgment of boundaries in his mother, who broke convention by being an educated, independent, well-traveled, and enterprising young lady in the old-fashioned South of the early 1900s. The same traits were instilled in Uncle John and my grandfather, who were never formally disciplined by their parents. The two kids never heard the word *no* from their parents. To some people, this would appear to be a child-rearing debacle in which the inmates ran the asylum. Instead, my great-grandmother's laissez-faire parenting approach developed two wildly curious and intelligent overachievers who excelled at everything they got their hands on.

Uncle John always told us that as children, if he or my grandfather ever had a question for their mother about how something worked or why something was the way it was, she generally did not give them a full answer. Instead, they would walk into the house a day or two later and discover that a book about the subject had been placed on the table for them to read. One notable instance of the boys' curiosity at work was when they became interested in electricity at the respective ages of 11 and 14. My great-grandmother was accommodating and informed them that she had set aside some space in the attic for them to carry out their experiments. With my grandfather spearheading the experiment, the boys gathered all the books available from the library, a host of electric coils, and other devices and proceeded to reroute electricity from the house into their "laboratory." They boast that at one point they had harnessed and conducted 10,000 volts of electricity into that small space. Always making practical use of his knowledge, my grandfather took his new skills and wired some of my great-grandfather's rental properties for the tenants. All this may seem unusual, and it was at the time, but to my grandfather and Uncle John it was just a part of their childhood.

Another striking example of the boys' ingenuity occurred around the time my grandfather was 10 years old and constructed a radio from scratch. Late in the afternoon many of the local farmers would gather and listen to the boys' homemade radio, not quite sure what to make of the small electric box that "pulled voices out of the air."

This practice of putting no limits on my grandfather and Uncle John's curiosity and ambitions translated into a "can do" attitude in the boys. They hardly stopped with conducting electricity, building radios, or rebuilding cars. The two boys took the same attitude toward their formal education. By the time Uncle John was in high school and thinking about college, that sense of adventure and the self-reliant attitude instilled in him by his mother directed his sights far from home. Since my grandfather was a few years older and had begun college at Georgia Tech but then transferred to Yale, Uncle John wanted to pursue an Ivy League education too. The story goes that when the two brothers were young boys, my grandfather once asked an old farmer in

Winchester which school he believed was the best college in the country. The farmer's simple response was "Yale."

Under normal circumstances Uncle John would have had no trouble obtaining entrance to Yale, having gotten A's in every course he took, but after studying admission materials around his freshman year in high school, he realized that it appeared impossible for a child at Winchester High School to gain admission. The problem was that the high school in Winchester did not offer the required four years of math. Never one to hear the word *no* on the path to achieving a goal, Uncle John approached the principal of the high school. When the principal heard about Uncle John's quandary, he told him that he had no problem with the idea of a fourth-year math class; however, they had no students and no teacher for the class. The principal explained to Uncle John that they needed at least eight students to begin the class and of course needed a teacher. Uncle John's response: "No problem; I'll teach the class."

Uncle John found eight friends willing to take the class and persuaded the principal to allow him to teach the class. From there Uncle John both taught and took the class and passed the exams administered by the principal. His favorite quip from the experience was that "all my students passed." Passing the course was the final leg to admission at Yale since he had chosen to take the college entrance exams in annual stages at the conclusion of each high school year at Vanderbilt University in Nashville rather than in one sitting (like today's SAT).

Although my great-grandmother's constant provision of book knowledge and the concept of self-empowerment played an important role in her children's development, she left another great and lasting impression on her sons: her desire to travel and seek new adventures. Around the time Uncle John was 12 and my grandfather was 15, Vella decided it was time for a trip. That summer they loaded up the car and took off for two months. Set on exploring the northeastern United States, they visited Washington, D.C.; Philadelphia; and New York. During the trip they often camped out along the way, prepared their own meals, and listed all the sites and museums they would visit. A few years later, Vella took the boys off on another two-month adventure during the summer, but this time they set out to explore all the great sites west of the Mississippi, including the national parks and the Pacific Ocean. This sense of adventure and willingness to travel stuck with Uncle John his entire life. As an adult he returned the favor by taking his own children and his nephews and nieces, including my father, on trips, including one across Europe. Just as his mother had done, Uncle John placed the children in charge and gave them many critical responsibilities, such as holding and keeping track of the money for the trip, mapping the day's course, and selecting lodging. In many ways, the spirit of traveling is a lasting heritage from Vella in our family as nearly every Templeton I know possesses a similar desire to see different parts of the world and have adventures.

After Uncle John attended Yale and completed a Rhodes scholarship to Balliol College in Oxford, he and a friend set out from Oxford on a trip around the world, intending to visit 35 nations. In true Templeton fashion, this trip was planned on a tight budget; nearly half of the 200 British pounds they set out with came from poker winnings Uncle John had socked away at Oxford. Despite the small budget, Uncle John was a consummate planner and had mapped out the entire trip in advance, including parceling out the funds for each segment of the journey. Taking the idea a bit further, he then mailed the appropriate budgeted amounts to their future locations in an attempt to maintain strict discipline in their spending. During his travels Uncle

John toured history in the making as their stop in Berlin brought them face to face with the building power of Nazis at the 1936 Olympics. His trip continued across Europe, through the Middle East, and then into Asia, including stops in India, China, and Japan. What is most instructive here is not simply that Uncle John had the curiosity and took the initiative to see all those places but what he did while he traveled. In keeping with the formula applied many years earlier during travels with his mother, Uncle John turned traveling into an intense learning experience. He studied the locations and their history, the people and their customs, and the museums; it was in fact a deeply educational experience. Because he threw himself into the culture and researched the locations and people ahead of time, he completed the trip with a bedrock of geopolitical knowledge in place.

This is yet another important stop in our journey through what made Uncle John the investor he would become. Before Uncle John's launching of his Templeton investment funds and persisting at least until a few decades ago, there was a sentiment in investing that the only stocks worth buying were in the United States. Of course, having been so well traveled and therefore more knowledgeable about the broader world, he saw this widespread belief system among U.S. investors as pure folly. However, depending on who you asked, there were any number of reasons why this was the investing paradigm. When Uncle John was at Yale, his fellow students were generally well off and many were personally invested in stocks. When Uncle John asked them why they bought only U.S. stocks, the usual response was that the United States was the only country that mattered.

Uncle John always remarked that he found that behavior arrogant and shortsighted. Over the many years that followed some of that original arrogance among U.S. investors became less outspoken, but biases against foreign investing have lingered at a lower level. In later years the justifications were not understanding foreign accounting rules and choosing to invest in a U.S. multinational company to gain exposure to foreign economies. In sum, this collective set of biased reasoning represented the *majority* wisdom for many decades over Uncle John's career. Not that he minded too much. Trust me; he is unflinching when he sees an opportunity to take advantage of human ignorance or misconceptions in the stock market. To Uncle John investing in bargain stocks from other nations was only common sense. The particular country mattered no more than did the particular neighborhood in New York where he found the $200 sofa bed for $5, as long as it was truly a bargain.

The notion of investing globally today is taken for granted, and the mutual fund world is now full of managers buying stocks in Europe, Asia, South America, and just about everywhere under the sun. If you investigate these funds, it should not come as a surprise that many carry the Templeton name. The point is that even back in the first half of the twentieth century, when no one else bought foreign stocks, Uncle John was comfortable investing in other countries because he had taken the time to become knowledgeable rather than be guided by biases. Perhaps it was harder or a bigger challenge to research a stock in Japan in the early 1960s. It was also a bigger challenge to attend Yale instead of a closer reputable school such as Vanderbilt, coming out of Winchester, Tennessee.

The truth is that Uncle John became knowledgeable about foreign countries because he was taught at an early age to pursue knowledge without regard to boundaries. Unfounded biases and prejudices lead to ignorance, and ignorance is a handicap in every walk of life. The constant give-and-take between Uncle John's curiosity and the knowledge he sought to feed it accelerated his learning curve over the course of his life and eventually complemented his innate wisdom.

If there is one thread that stretches throughout Uncle John's investing career, it is his ability to sit back and act with wisdom, not just smarts, although he has plenty of those too. When Uncle John was a young child, friends and acquaintances of his mother always said the same thing about him, which was that he was "born old." The character trait that people saw in him as a young child was a unique blend of common sense and wisdom for someone with very little life experience. Incidentally, that is what enables him to play a cool hand when it comes to the markets. It sounds so simple: Because he possesses innate wisdom and calmness, he is routinely able to see things that others cannot. The fact is that it is simple but extremely uncommon.

When emotions or popular misconceptions guide the stock market into a crash or a bubble, as they periodically do, simple wisdom cannot be found in the collective action of the buyers and sellers in the market. In other words, it is easy for others to minimize his common sense and wisdom in hindsight when nearly all observers are behaving under a rational, objective mindset. Many investors say that they are anxious for a big sell-off in the stock market so that they can pick up bargains. The facts state the case differently, though, when we see the Dow Jones fall 22.6 percent in a single day. Where were all those enthusiastic buyers when the Dow carried a price/earnings (P/E) ratio of 6.8 in 1979 and stayed at those low levels for a few years? What we find when we ask these questions is that buying stocks when no one else will is difficult for the majority of investors. Incidentally, that is the best way to get a bargain, and getting a bargain leads to the best returns.

Although it is false etymology to characterize a bear market with the downward swatting motion of that animal, let us use that image for the sake of humor (the term supposedly comes from stock jobbers in London selling bearskins before they owned them, or short selling). If most investors think they can stand in the path of a bear raising its arm to swat them, they are probably wrong. However, Uncle John basically sees the bear as swinging its arm back to slap him a high five because he knows that stocks are about to get a lot cheaper and present more bargains for purchasers.

It is all a matter of *perspective*, and Uncle John's perspective on the market is very unusual despite how simple it appears. Consider this type of perspective in Uncle John's own words: "People are always asking me where the outlook is good, but that's the wrong question. The right question is: Where is the outlook most miserable?" The obvious application of this concept in practice is avoid following the crowd. The crowd in this case consists of the majority of buyers in the stock market who continuously flock to the stocks whose prospects look the best. Avoiding situations in which the prospects look the best is counterintuitive to the way we conduct our normal day-to-day lives. We look for jobs in promising fields; we go outside on sunny days. Oddly, this behavior translates poorly into investment success. Instead, the opposite behavior is required, that is, seeking out poor outlooks (that have potential to improve).

Being able to act in this manner requires investors to separate themselves from the crowd, even physically. In his early years Uncle John managed money in New York, as was the custom, but when he relocated to the Bahamas in 1968, he soon obtained the best record as a mutual fund manager. It was not a coincidence. Uncle John always remarks that his results improved after he moved to Nassau because he was forced to think far differently than the rest of Wall Street. From that point on he was not seeing the same company presentations and attending the same events as all the other analysts on Wall Street. Once he removed himself from that environment, his own thinking took full control, and that made all the difference. Some readers may think harder about the benefits of this physical and mental separation when they remember that Warren Buffett lives in Omaha, Nebraska.

Uncle John's ability to take advantage of the market's occasional folly or naive misconceptions was honed throughout his childhood and into his college years by sitting at, of all places, the poker table. Uncle John in his earlier days was an expert poker player, or at the very least he was an expert compared to the boys in Winchester and, later, Yale and Oxford. Uncle John learned the game of poker around the age of eight and often played for pennies. Later, when he was at Yale, heading into his sophomore year in 1931, he was faced with the same general misfortune that was afflicting the entire country at that time; the Great Depression was well under way. It was in that year that my great-grandfather informed Uncle John that he no longer could support his college education, not even to the amount of one dollar, given the dire circumstances of the economy.

Luckily for Uncle John, his uncle, Watson Templeton, offered him $200 for the trip back to Yale so that he could attempt to pay his own way through school. Uncle John graciously accepted the offer and promptly set out for Yale, determined to find enough work and per-haps some financial aid. He was able to obtain both but needed more funds to cover the cost of his education. This time he turned to the poker table, where his skills in tracking the cards that had been played, assessing probability, and sizing up the abilities and strategies of oth-ers paid off big. Uncle John estimates that as much as 25 percent of his education funding came from playing poker. The remaining 75 percent came from working student jobs and obtaining academic scholarships because of his high grades.

The tales of Uncle John's poker playing take on a special light when we frame them in the context of investing. Uncle John's mastery of poker is interesting because that game requires superior acumen in probability, risk taking, and, perhaps most important, psychology. It is not unusual to meet professional investors who are skilled in the technical aspects of finance, accounting, or economics. In fact, the world is full of smart people who can deconstruct an income statement, balance sheet, and statement of cash flows; apply aspects of microeconomics such as competitive strategy; sniff out accounting gimmicks; assign an intrinsic value to a company; and so on. At the same time, the ingredient needed to transform someone from just another smart guy or gal into a successful investor is the ability not to act foolishly.

Seems simple, right? Think again. Very much of what it takes to be successful in poker is also what it takes to be successful in investing. You need the ability to understand the motive or the driving force behind the actions you are witnessing. Let's say you are playing poker with the same group of friends as always and one player has a habit of bluffing under certain circumstances. Since you have learned to spot this player's bluffs, you usually can wait until he confidently raises the pot and then call when you are ready to take all of his money. Well, you cannot exactly call someone's hand in the stock market, but if a stock is trading at an exorbitant level in comparison to its measures of prospective earnings, cash flows, and the like, you can conclude that the market for that stock, like your friend, is a bit full of it. In that case, you can be assured that your friend eventually will lose his shirt; and similarly, the market for that expensive stock will fall when investors figure out they are holding not a full house but a pair of threes. We also should note that in the time leading up to the end of your friend's charade, he has been winning hand after hand and rubbing it in everyone's face. To put it all in perspective, Uncle John is the player at the table who at the beginning of the night detected the bluff and patiently waited to take your friend's money. Now that we have explored this stock market paradigm, let us revisit our original point.

To make the jump from just another smart guy or gal placing money in the stock market to a successful investor requires a little something extra, and that something is called good judgment. For what it is worth, Uncle John believes that his judgment sets him apart from other investors. Never mind his Ivy League education, Rhodes scholarship, gift with numbers and concepts, and so forth. He credits his judgment as one of the main differentiating factors in his success rate. Incidentally, one of Uncle John's favorite poems is "If" by Rudyard Kipling. For those who do not recall, the poem begins "If you can keep your head when all about you are losing theirs…" Uncle John has always possessed this uncanny ability to not lose his cool. Coincidentally, "If" was one of my favorites as a young child also. One fine example of Uncle John keeping a cool head came from an experience while a student at Yale. Because Uncle John was working his way through school, he required a bank checking account for his funds. Like many others during the Great Depression, however, he learned firsthand the pain of depositing money, only to watch the bank that was holding his funds turn insolvent and go bankrupt. Never one to throw in the towel, he stayed the course and continued working (and playing poker) to remain in school. The second time depositing funds, however, he sought the counsel of one of his professors to place his deposit in the safest bank in New Haven. After receiving this advice he took his money to the bank and made his deposit. Only a few weeks later, though, he was walking down the street and saw a long line of people extended down the sidewalk of his "safe" bank, demanding their money. He calmly walked over to the line and confirmed that the bank was indeed experiencing a run. While doing so, he noticed that all of the depositors were standing in line at the checking accounts window, while no one was in line at the savings account window. Always one to remain calm and think on his feet, he walked up to the savings account window, transferred his checking account into a savings account, and withdrew his money.

The key takeaway from our discussion of Uncle John's investing judgment is that this represents an important realization to those who wish to invest successfully in the stock market. The truth is that if you have the wisdom to purchase investments, even simple, reputable, low-charge mutual funds, when everyone in the market is scared and complaining about how bad things look, you already have the tools necessary to achieve above-average results. Remember what we said earlier. This is a tough thing to admit because your authors are professional money managers too, but the truth is that there are plenty of smart fund managers out there whom you can trust with your savings (there are some bad ones too, so do your homework!). If you can understand the benefit of buying a farm at auction for mere cents on the dollar and understand that it is going for cents on the dollar because no one else is there to bid up the price, you get the concept of bargain hunting in the stock market. However, if the courthouse steps are full of bidders shoving each other and screaming bids to higher and higher levels, it is probable that you are not going to get a good bargain. The important thing to remember is that if you buy and sell stocks, mutual funds, or anything else in the same fashion as everyone else, your returns will be just like everyone else's. So "if you can keep your head when all about you are losing theirs," you are well on your way to investing wisely. However, consider this proposition in Uncle John's words rather than ours: "To buy when others are despondently selling and to sell when others are avidly buying requires the greatest fortitude and pays the greatest ultimate rewards."

Chapter | 2

THE FIRST TRADE IN
MAXIMUM PESSIMISM

*Bull markets are born on pessimism, grow on skepticism, mature
on optimism, and die on euphoria. The time of maximum
pessimism is the best time to buy, and the time of maximum
optimism is the best time to sell.*
—Sir John Templeton, February 1994

The year was 1939, and despite a brief pause in the economic
malaise from 1935 to 1937, the U.S. economy had been treading
water since October 29, 1929. In short, the Great Depression had persisted for a decade, and the psychological turmoil that accompanied
rampant unemployment, homelessness, and even the inability to
secure a hot meal was never far from the public's consciousness. In
1938, a resurgence of economic activity in the previous two years had
proved temporary, and the slump had returned. Adding to concerns
was the possibility of a full-blown world war born in Europe. The end
result was a decade marked by erratic beliefs about the U.S. economy.
Moreover, the future of individual free will in Europe was being called
into question as the Nazis began to conquer that continent.

Not surprisingly, all these events found an open stage to play on in the U.S. stock market. If the first act brought hope, the second act followed with despair, and that back-and-forth between hope and despair took a toll over time. The constant fluctuation in the way investors perceived and interpreted the economic and geopolitical events unfolding before them produced *the most volatile decade of stock price changes ever,* according to research on the Dow Jones Industrial Average. What is so interesting about the crash in 1929 and often is overlooked is that the true carnage unfolded in the two years that followed. Nevertheless, most people who think about the stock market crash, the Depression, and the 1930s associate the period with miserable times in the market. However, Figure 2.1 clearly shows that depending on one's *perspective,* there were some pretty good times embedded in that period as well.

One of the most critical observations to be gleaned from our discussion of the stock market in the 1930s is the overall frequency of changes in the prices of stocks. Although some of the declines in stock prices were merited over this period—it was the Great Depression, after all—this raises an important question: Did the underlying value of the companies that those stocks represent also change with the same hyperactive frequency? The answer is no.

One of the key features of an asset bubble is that the market prices associated with the assets get much too high when the buyers are swept away by optimism and then later, after the market crashes, get much too low compared with the value of the assets as the sellers become pessimistic. This exaggerated rise and fall typified the years preceding and following the crash of 1929. Most important, this misbehavior of a stock price relative to the value of the company is not relegated to periods of market bubbles but can be a normal characteristic of daily, weekly, monthly, or yearly stock prices. If we could visualize this basic phe-

Figure 2.1

The Dow Jones Industrial Average, 1926–1940

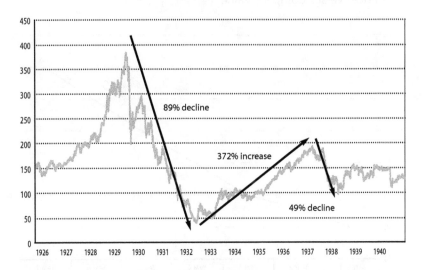

nomenon, it would look something like Figure 2.2. The notion that a company and the stock price that supposedly represents its value in the market can become divorced from each other has its popular roots in the work and writings of Benjamin Graham, the coauthor of *Security Analysis*. Graham postulated, correctly in our opinion, that every company has an intrinsic value; in other words, every company can be assigned a reasonable estimate of what it is worth. However, in spite of this, the market for a company's stock can fluctuate independently of the company's value.

As we can see in this oversimplified figure, the company's value depicted by the solid line continues to increase over time. This company sells more products year after year and over the years continues to find ways to increase the amount of money brought in on an annual basis for its owners. In the meantime, the stock market's enthusiasm for the company ebbs and flows as buyers and sellers of the stock change their opinion about the company for any number of reasons.

Figure 2.2

Stock Prices versus Company Value

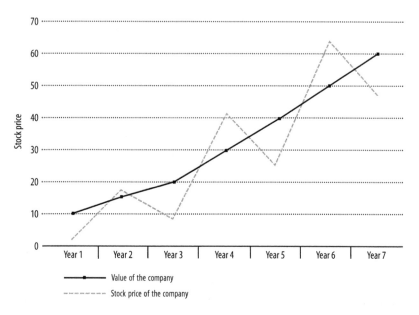

We also should point out that these assessments are made on a daily basis. Does the value of a company change on a daily basis? No, but that does not prevent the buyers and sellers of stocks from sizing it up it on a daily basis. Even more important, sometimes buyers and sellers are guided by decision-making factors that have little to do with the company itself. The scenarios are not hard to imagine. Perhaps investors have found a more exciting company to own, or perhaps they are upset that the company will earn less money than they expected in a particular year. It is important to realize that people in the stock market sell the stocks they own for reasons that sometimes have little or nothing to do with what they suppose a company is worth. Sometimes they sell the stocks they own simply because they observe others selling them in the market, giving no consideration to the value of the company. Sometimes buyers purchase shares because they see other buyers driving up the price. Uncle John always said, "Sometimes the cause of higher prices is higher prices." The point is that if you have some notion that stock prices always accurately reflect the true worth of the company, you are in for the manic ride of your life. Rather than buy stocks, take your money and spend it at Disneyland; you will have much more fun on those rides.

As you might have guessed by this point, we recommend buying stocks when their prices decline below the value of the company a stock represents. As a simple example, Company A, including all its plants, inventory, finished products, employees, and so on, would be offered at $100 if its operator tallied it up into one number and tried to sell it to you, but the stock price is quoted at $75. Taking it a step further, if the company today is worth $100 and the stock price is quoted at $100 but you think the company will be worth $200 in a few years, all the better. In either case, buy the stock and wait for the market to figure out what you know, which is what the company is worth or will be worth in terms of its prospects.

This relationship is at the core of value investing: buying things for less than they are worth. That is the idea. As you will come to see later, you can arrive at this conclusion from a number of different directions. Most important, this strategy should permeate all your investing, whether you are dealing in stocks, real estate, or even art, baseball cards, or stamps. Identifying a discrepancy between what an asset is worth and its market price is the name of the game in every case. Just remember that in each case the price of something and the value of that thing can be far different. From here on, we will refer to this practice of buying things for less than they are worth as finding a bargain. Our next mission is to install you into the club of bargain hunters.

Uncle John once remarked that observing, as a young man, that the behavior of stock prices can differ greatly from the value of the companies they represent prompted him to enter the investment counsel business in 1937. He understood early on that a stock and a company are two different things. Although one is supposed to represent the value of the other, it is common for stock prices and the value of an ongoing company to become disconnected and differ. A lot of people say they understand this, but it is common to see investors, even experienced ones, confuse a company with its stock. Most often this confusion is exposed when someone, such as a broker, an analyst, or a self-proclaimed "expert," discusses "a stock" on television, on the phone, in research reports, in blogs, or even at a cocktail party. If you observe them closely, they talk only about the company itself despite the fact that the *stock price* and its relation to the company's value and future profits are far more important considerations.

The reason behind this is probably people's innate affinity for storytelling and accumulating and then sharing knowledge. Companies are easy to talk about in story form and translate well into future conversations with others. "I invested in this company, and it is going to reinvent the market for footwear." Statements like this are common. They can be exciting, and they stroke our egos and make us feel smart in conversation. However, these statements can cause us to buy overvalued stocks and pay commissions to the brokers who spread the stories. Fanciful or catchy stories about companies and their accompanying popularity often lead to an investing disaster.

This is not to say that the brokers who share the stories or the analysts who generate the stories want to mislead you. That is usually not the case. Rather, you must understand that they are under great pressure to create something akin to a "sales pitch" to be bounced off investors around the world. Their bosses compel them to talk about things that get investors' attention, and interesting companies and their vibrant prospects go a lot further in that effort than stale reams of statistics, ratios, data, and calculations of a company's fair value: the things that matter most in the investment decision process. Wall Street brokers supply what the majority of investors actually demand: intelligent stories about a company's prospects for the next three months to a year. Those stories and their ability to feed an investor's imagination can guide stock prices higher or lower.

Bargain hunters should never adopt a one-stop investment strategy that is based on well-told stories whether the stories come from your neighbor, your barber, or the smartest analyst on Wall Street. Bargain hunters must rely on their own assessment of whether the stock price is far enough below what they believe a company is worth. This is the sole guiding light on the horizon, and skepticism is the compass. Buying stocks solely on the basis of stories about companies is like letting the mythological sirens entice you onto the rocks of the shoreline. That rocky shoreline is scattered with the bodies of investors who listen to stories.

This raises a good question, which is how to identify a story stock and avoid buying it. In this case, numbers do not lie. Take a look at the stock price divided by its sales per share, its earnings per share, or its book value per share. If this calculated number comes back significantly higher than that of its competitors or its relevant stock market index, chances are that you have found an overly popular story stock. Do not take our word for it, though. A tremendous body of research conducted over the last 50 years empirically confirms that stocks carrying a high ratio of price to sales, price to earnings, or price to book value make bad investments over the long run. So much previous work has been done on this subject that it would be wasteful to reinvent the wheel and reprint it in this chapter. There are some easily accessible, well-written books that detail these statistical studies and what your long-term prospects are if you are a purchaser of popular companies whose stocks display these characteristics. Often these popular companies have stocks that are the most expensive in the market. That is, if you rank all the companies in the stock market by their respective ratios of price to sales, price to earnings, and price to book, from highest to lowest, the stocks at the top of the list often are some of the most popular companies in the market.

The research shows that routinely purchasing these stocks leads to performance that is less than the average of the market. In other words, you may beat the odds for a while, but you are destined to fail. Armed with this knowledge, why would you ever purchase these stocks? It makes no sense to tilt the empirical probabilities built into the market against yourself. Beating the stock market over long periods is not easy, and avoiding the purchase of stocks destined to fall in price is the first step toward accomplishing this feat. Simply avoiding these stocks raises the probability that you will be successful.

Finally, the fact that these high-ratio stocks are attached to companies with the brightest *known* prospects is not a coincidence. At the same time, if you scanned your list of stocks ranked from the highest to lowest ratios of price to sales, price to earnings, price to book, and price to cash flow, you might discover that at the bottom of the list are some of the most unattractive, unexciting companies in the market. Perversely, these companies have been proven over time to have the most rewarding stocks you can purchase. If you chose to focus only on the bottom 10 percent of that list for an investment, you would be increasing the probability of your success as an investor a great deal. Careful bargain hunters find that the bottom of this barrel is a fertile hunting ground for successful stock investments.

When you try to decipher whether a stock is a bargain or is fairly priced, you will need to get some information on the company so that you can understand the business, measure its performance over time and in relation to its competitors, and learn what has caused the stock to lose favor. Brokers' reports often include some of this basic factual information. Uncle John never had a problem using brokers' reports to gather background information on a company, its competitors, its industry, and so on. Always heed his basic advice on using this information: If you are reading something in a research report, that information already is included in the stock price. Getting hold of those reports is not the equivalent of receiving tomorrow's newspaper today, and you are not reading them in a vacuum.

After all this discussion about the separation of the stock price from the value of a company, let us digress for a moment. Not every change in a stock's price is unwarranted, and the values of companies can and do change over time. This can occur quickly in some instances. If your company makes buggy whips, on the day Henry Ford rolls out the Model T on an assembly line, the value of your business will change very fast (your product is obsolete). If your company has a mountain of loans and the lenders decide they do not want to do business with you anymore, the value of your business will change very fast (you are headed toward bankruptcy). What these examples show is that in each case in which a stock price changes dramatically, you must be an active processor of the information that led to the change. It is not prudent to purchase stocks only because they have fallen in price. In fact, that would be reckless and lead to unsatisfactory investment results.

More often than not, the changing conditions in a business—higher or lower sales, rising or declining expenses, stronger or weaker cash flows—that alter the true worth of a company are years in the making. Despite this, the stock prices that represent the supposed long-term worth of businesses to the market are controlled by people who are subject to daily changes of emotion and on occasion are guided by their emotions in the decision-making process. Everyone can point to a rash decision he or she made in some walk of life outside investing that was guided by emotions. The point is that this rash behavior can extend into the stock market, and it produces by far the best opportunities for bargain hunters to purchase cheap stocks. In most cases, when the moment passes, we come to our senses and realize our folly. Your steadfast mission as a bargain hunter is never to make an investment decision in which emotion plays a role. Instead, your task is to take advantage of the misjudgment of others when they act rashly. The old saying is that hindsight is 20/20. Bargain hunters must strive for 20/20 vision at all times rather than replicate easily avoided mistakes that resulted from emotion or poor judgment. Uncle John made his career by taking advantage of people with less than clear thinking, purchasing the stocks they recklessly sold in haste, often on the basis of emotion.

You can be sure that these events are periodic and will occur over and over. Overreacting to a situation is the way humans are wired, but lifelong experience in a number of situations aids us in dealing with similar situations more rationally. For instance, if we get a cut on the hand, we instinctively react to stop the bleeding. When people start to lose money in a stock, they instinctively "stop the bleeding" by selling the stock. There's no way around that knee-jerk reaction, but it is often the wrong response when one is investing in stocks. In life, we routinely get cuts on our hands, and over the years it gets easier to distinguish a bad cut from a minor scratch. That's why few people scream their way to the emergency room if they get a paper cut. People's lifelong history of dealing with cuts enables them to size up their severity quickly.

Conversely, not everyone has a commensurate level of experience in handling stocks, particularly ones that are dropping in price. In the stock market, people go screaming to the emergency room with a mere paper cut. Some are oblivious to the possibility of a cut until it happens. They simply overreact to what they are seeing and focus on the loss of money rather than the more important factor: the increasing attraction of the stock price at lower levels. When investors overreact to bad news and sell their stocks off feverishly, they are increasing the inventory of bargains for you to choose from; this is the perspective of a bargain hunter. As a successful bargain hunter, it is to your advantage to have emotional sellers in the market because they create opportunities. Similarly, it is to your advantage to have sellers in the market who are guided solely by the news headlines, the charts they look at, superstition, "hot tips," or anything else that diverts them from investing on the basis of the stock price relative to a company's fair value. The point is that these misguided participants are in the market and should be thought of as your friends. They will create bargain opportunities for you as well as the best returns after you purchase shares. In Uncle John's words (tongue in cheek), these are the very people you want to help. Your role as a bargain hunter is to accommodate them by offering to buy the stocks they are desperate to sell and sell them the stocks they are desperate to buy.

Uncle John has the benefit of seven decades of experience in the market. His accumulation of experiences has made spotting bargains in the stock market second nature for him. We noticed throughout our time investing under him that he kept getting better with each year he continued to invest.

As you may have gathered by now, the basic reality is that bargain hunters most often look to purchase a company whose problems have been exposed to the stock market. Investors' recognition of these problems is usually what caused the stock market to sell the stock and drop its price. Through the experience of assessing many companies and their problems over and over, you too will learn to distinguish small problems from big problems and take advantage of situations in which the stock market has overreacted to a small problem that a company may be facing. One example could be a company that is building a new plant that it will use to sell more widgets. The company has told investors and analysts that the plant will be up and running in a year's time, and the company will sell 25 percent more goods once it is running. The analysts have planned on and calculated the probable sales of the new plant and built it into their earnings forecasts for the coming year. Unfortunately, construction of the plant has stalled, and the company now says that the plant will take six months longer to get up and running than originally was planned. The analysts reduce their estimates, and the buyers of the stock are caught off guard by the announcement and sell the stock immediately, driving the price down 30 percent over the next few weeks. The question here is, is this problem temporary, and will it be fixed? If the answer is yes, this is a good example of how to take advantage of a small problem that led to a big overreaction. To a long-term owner the company is not worth 30 percent less; it may take only a little while longer for the new sales to materialize. Taking advantage of big overreactions in a stock price caused by temporary problems at a company is a bread-and-butter tactic for bargain hunters.

Understanding the history of the market is a huge asset for investing. This is the case not because events repeat themselves exactly but because patterns of events and the way the people who make up the market react can be typical and predictable. History shows that people overreact to surprises in the stock market. They always have and always will. Grasping that fact sets the table for bargain hunters to scoop up cheap stocks when a surprise occurs, and anticipating and looking forward to these surprises provides bargain hunters with the mindset to act decisively when the opportunity arrives. Salivating for a big surprise that sends stocks into a frenzied sell-off is a common daydream for bargain hunters.

Despite Uncle John's experience, time, and cumulative observations, he actually was capitalizing on these behavioral observations in his earliest years of investing, and that is good news for the rest of us. Investors who understand that this type of rash behavior occurs in the stock market and leads to opportunity already have an edge.

Sometimes it helps to view this volatile market behavior in a simpler framework. Let's say that for several years you have been operating a successful lemonade stand in your neighborhood during the summer. You are approaching your teens and think you might like to get into something more sophisticated, such as mowing lawns. You realize that your lemonade stand can turn a decent profit on a hot sunny day. In your experience, you can rake in about $200 in sales over the course of a summer (hey, every capitalist starts somewhere). You think, well, I have so many customers from around the neighborhood who every summer stop by for a lemonade; they would be disappointed to see the business go. An idea strikes you: I'll sell the lemonade stand to my friend next door so that it will continue in business. I can sell him the stand, lemonade powder, and jugs of distilled water. Also, since it is such a steady, dependable business, I'll bet I can persuade my friend to pay a little something above those costs since I can promise him he will make his money back very quickly from my loyal customers.

You approach your friend with your proposition that he buy the lemonade stand, and immediately he blurts out, "I love lemonade! I've been saving some money for a while, and I would love to buy your stand—I'll make a killing! I'll give you my $100 for your lemonade stand." You, being a bit more grounded, say, "Okay, before you do that, how about you come out next weekend and watch me run the stand on Saturday? I'll introduce you to my customers, and you'll get a feel for the business. That way, you will have a better idea of what you are buying." It's agreed; you part ways until Saturday.

In the meantime, your friend, who is a bit of a showboat, goes to school and brags to all his friends about the lemonade stand he will purchase from you during the coming weekend. His classmates are all big lemonade drinkers and happen to like your lemonade the best. They get excited, and some devise their own plans to show up Saturday and offer more than $100 for the stand. Saturday comes around, and your friend shows up as expected, on time. It is a bit cooler than normal that day and overcast as well. Within five minutes of your friend's arrival a pack of bicycles comes racing up the street toward the stand, and you can hear those nine rowdy kids screaming from a quarter of a mile away. As they pull up to the stand and toss their bikes to the ground, your friend, realizing what is going on, says, "Well, a deal is a deal. How about I give you that $100 for the lemonade stand?" Faster than you can open your mouth, another kid blurts out, "Hey, I've got $110 I'll give you!" Yet another screams, "I've got $120!" The girl with pigtails kicks him in the groin and screams "I have $125!" The neighborhood bully elbows past her and says "Here's $150!"

You are a bit surprised but are more than happy to accommodate the potential owners. As you open your mouth to take the bully's deal, a funny thing happens. A raindrop hits the stand, and as you look up, the bully is already on his bike, booking it back home. A few more drops come. You look to the girl who offered $125, and she's halfway down the block screaming about her new clothes getting wet. The kid who offered $120 pauses for a moment, looks at you and the others, and boldly says, "A little drizzle doesn't scare me." The muffled rumble of distant thunder is heard in the background, and he turns pale and jumps for his bike. In the meantime you begin to cover your stand with the tarps you pack so that your products won't get damaged.

The kid who offered $110 and his three friends huddle together to decide whether they want to make an offer for your business; a debate ensues among them. You hear one say, "Hey, that girl who just left makes straight A's in class, and she probably knows something we don't. She did not make an offer. I think buying this stand may be a bad idea." Another one says, "My feet are getting wet. Nobody said anything about my feet getting wet; this is more than I signed up for. This lemonade business looks like a stupid idea; we should be selling umbrellas—it's raining, for crying out loud. Let's get into the umbrella business, not lemonade! There's a pile of old ones in our garage that we can use our money to buy from my parents, and I'm sure we can sell them. Let's get into the umbrella business!" Collectively, that group walks away from your stand for their various reasons.

Last but not least your friend from next door, the one who wants to buy your stand for $100, is looking a bit soggy and depressed as the rain comes down harder. You ask him if everything is okay. He says, "Well, everyone else who was here has left but me. Everyone else is probably right; this is a bad idea. You know, what if it rains every Saturday? You haven't had a single customer today. If it rains every Saturday this summer, we would never make a sale, and I'd be out $100. I don't think I'm interested in buying your stand anymore; it's a scary business and obviously a risky one too. Besides, you saw that no one else likes it either; they must be right. If the sun doesn't come out again on a Saturday, I'll be ruined." He slumps off toward his bike, pulls it up, and strides off down the road.

As he rides off, you look across the street, and a kid who is sitting alone under a tree with a raincoat on starts to stroll over to your stand. It's still raining, but not quite as hard. You look at him and say, "Hey, you're a pretty smart kid; you brought a raincoat today." The kid cracks a smile and says, "Yes, I check the weather often before I go out to play, and the weatherman said there was a chance of a thunderstorm today." As he's talking, your mind starts churning: All right, maybe this kid wants to buy the stand. He is still here, after all, and every other kid has left to go home. Before you can introduce the idea, the kid looks at you and says, "I overheard at lunch last week that you were selling your lemonade stand this Saturday, and I thought I'd come out and watch to see how it went." He continues: "I see that the other kids left and there are no other buyers. Maybe I can take it off your hands since you would like to get out of the lemonade business." You say, "Okay, what's your offer?" Calmly, the kid looks at you and says, "I'll give you $50." Your jaw drops. "Fifty dollars?!? My inventory of powders and water alone costs $50! You'd be getting the rest of the business for free!" The kid looks at you and says, "Well, it appears I am the only buyer out here, and my offer is $50 to own your business." You look at him, a bit frustrated, and say, "I do want to sell it and you are the only buyer left, so I guess it's only fair that I sell it to you for $50." You shake on it.

Before you can ask if he needs to go home to get his money, he reaches deep into the pocket of his weathered hand-me-down raincoat and pulls out a wad of cash the size of a bullfrog, bound by an old dirty rubber band. This also makes you uncomfortable, thinking that maybe this kid is a bit smarter than he let on. At any rate, you take the $50 and transfer ownership of the lemonade stand to the kid in the raincoat. Within 30 seconds of shaking on the deal, that pack of kids runs by with arms full of umbrellas and screams at the kid who just bought your stand: "Hey, kid! You must be some kind of idiot to buy that lemonade stand! What are you thinking?"

What we just described is a typical course of events that plays out over and over in the stock market. That is, a group of individuals bring their money and opinions into the stock of a specific company and then bid the price of that stock up and down on the basis of events that unfold in front of them. What is perhaps most notable is that so few of the buyers and sellers in our story applied sound reasoning or logic in the decision-making process. Instead, they reacted to the other buyers around the stand or the negative surprise of a rainstorm. In the meantime an informed observer who had studied the subject ahead of time and anticipated a distinct probability of rain was able to harness that event and its effect on the remaining buyers and sellers into buying an asset for much less than it was worth under normal circumstances. Importantly, the child bought the lemonade stand in the face of an overwhelming consensus among other children that it was a bad idea.

Bargain hunters who consistently buy stocks for less than they are worth need to get used to the idea of people not confirming or agreeing with their actions. As a matter of common sense, the only way a stock price can fall substantially is for people to sell the stock, and the primary reason people sell stocks is that the stocks have become unpopular. The best bargain hunters do not need confirmation from a multitude of others that they are correct to buy a stock. To buy something unpopular, you must be independent-minded and capable of relying on your own judgment. To some, such as Uncle John, this character trait is simply a part of who they are; for others, it must be learned.

The last point about the lemonade stand story is the importance of studying the situation ahead of time. It is a simple fact that people tend to panic when they are caught off guard. This happens in the stock market all the time. You cannot identify, predict, and prepare for every little risk you may face in the future. However, you can prepare for common types of events. In the case of the lemonade stand, some rain on a Saturday was a pretty run-of-the-mill event that should have been anticipated. The truth is that every business in the world has at least an occasional rainy day and every stock in the market that trades for less than it is worth has a rain cloud hovering over it. All businesses face problems. It is very important that you understand the nature of the rain cloud and what type of risks it poses. Is the rain a temporary setback, or are we running our lemonade stand too close to a creek that tends to flood and will wash our business away? There is no substitute for doing your homework when it comes to investing.

It is absolutely necessary to understand a business thoroughly before you buy its stock: how it works, what stimulates its sales activity, the types of pressures it faces to sustain profits, the fluctuation of its results over time, how it fares against its competition. Having this information is the best way to create a psychological fortress for decision making on a stock. This is the type of information you will need to process if you want to increase your accuracy in determining whether a bad situation is temporary or the business is about to be washed away forever by a flood. There is a risk of getting washed away; that can happen. The idea behind bargain hunting is to become not an unblinking contrarian but rather a wise buyer of out-of-favor stocks. Accumulating and processing this business information ahead of time will give you the conviction necessary to purchase a stock when it falls because the company had a rainy day. If you are going to invest in a situation in which the outlook is negative, you need to have the psychological fortitude to stand pat under the most imposing, darkest clouds and not run for the hills. In value investing, the price of success is paid in advance.

The lucky bidder for the lemonade stand prepared his new business the following Saturday morning for its first day of operation under his management. It appeared to be a much nicer day than the previous Saturday, and he noticed that the forecast was for a scorcher at around 90 degrees Fahrenheit. Little did he know that all around the neighborhood, parents and their children also had noticed the weather and were busy making plans for picnics, bike rides, games of touch football, and so on. As he set up the stand, he saw the group of kids with their umbrellas run by, screaming and bickering with one another over what to do with all their umbrellas on such a nice sunny day.

In the meantime a few customers arrive, and he makes a few sales. Before long, a line forms about 10 deep. Taking notice, some of the kids from last week's auction pull their bikes up to the stand. First, the seller's neighbor from next door pipes up, "Hey, the lemonade business isn't so bad after all; let me buy it from you for $100!" The kids with the umbrellas, proclaiming what a heck of a time it is to be in the lemonade business, throw their umbrellas down and erupt into the bidding: "No, forget that offer; we'll give you $120!" Miss Pigtails picks up a discarded umbrella and starts swinging it at those fools and screams, "I'll give you $150!" Not to be outdone, the neighborhood bully pushes them all aside and insists that the child accept his offer of $200 for the lemonade stand. After a quick glance around the stand to see that there is not a larger bully with more money to offer, the owner senses that it is an exceptional offer and quickly accepts the $200.

This Saturday proved to be a highly profitable adventure for the young lemonade stand owner. He purchased the lemonade stand for a mere $50 and a week later sold it for $200, making four times his original investment. During the span of a week, we must ask ourselves, what changed, if anything, to cause such a wide swing in the prices offered for the lemonade stand? Did the value of the lemonade stand change fourfold? Not at all; the only thing that changed was the onlookers' perception of the lemonade stand's value. In sum, the only variables that changed were the investing environment (from rainy to sunny) and the perceptions of the investors (from negative to positive). In this example, we can see what a powerful force investor *perception* is in the determination of asset prices. Some of the most dramatic changes in a stock's price often occur in the wake of these adjustments in investor perception rather than resulting from an actual change in the value of the asset.

As a successful bargain hunter, it is important that you learn to harness this energy of investor perception rather than get stampeded by it. One way to do this is to condition yourself to purchase stocks on rainy days in the market and sell them on sunny days. In doing so, you will find that the great majority of investors do the opposite. That is, they buy stocks on sunny days and sell them on rainy days. If they did not do this, stocks would not fall in price on the days when the outlook is less rosy. It sounds simple and commonsensical, but experience will show many bargain hunters that there is great psychological inertia that prevents investors from executing this task in real life.

With this primer out of the way, let us return to the year 1939. The health of the U.S. economy was once again debatable, and the stock market had highly variable perceptions of the war that had broken out in Europe. The interpretations of those events had turned negative during the last 12 months or so, and these views in the United States and Europe led the stock market down by 49 percent. Let us pause here and think about what we just said: Stock prices had fallen 49 percent in a mere 12 months! This should strike most clear-headed bargain hunters as a dramatic reassessment of the economy's prospects. Investors thought that the United States was dipping back into a depression and that the Nazis were going to destroy free will and the modern civilization that had sprung up in Europe. The consensus among investors in the United States was negative, and that belief was imposing its force on stocks, which were being sold off on the basis of the belief that more bad times would follow.

Despite this consensus view of fear for the worst, Uncle John had been observing these events quietly and was coming up with different conclusions on the probable course of future events. First, he already had developed some knowledge of Germany, its mindset, and the ferocity of its leaders. As we recall from Chapter 1, in the year that followed his study at Balliol College with his Rhodes scholarship, Uncle John traveled around the world on a shoestring budget with a friend from school. During this travel time in the early 1930s, he had been through Germany and even had attended the Olympic Games in Berlin, where he had seen firsthand the maladroit training, eerie conformity, and fervor that guided that group of people. Over the ensuing years, as the Nazis invaded one country after another and led Europe into a full-blown war after the invasion of Poland, he believed that the United States would get dragged into the war as well. On the basis of that supposition, he concluded that industrial firms in the United States would be pushed very hard to supply the commodities and goods to support U.S. entry into the war. In fact, he believed that even the most unexceptional, least efficient businesses would stand to benefit from the coming wave of economic activity.

This view came from his study of previous wars, such as the Civil War in the United States and World War I, which also stimulated demand for commodities. As the corporations and businesses in the United States scrambled to win contracts and supply the government with all the iron, steel, textiles, food, and so on, that would be needed, all those materials would require transportation from different parts of the country. From this simple observation, it appeared that railroad companies would benefit from the U.S. forces entering the war. In sum, whereas the stock market feared the threat of another downward economic spiral and the destruction of freedom in Europe, Uncle John saw a decent probability of future widespread economic stimuli as businesses all over the country responded to the call to war.

In a sense, you could say that Uncle John had an asymmetrical perspective on the future because of his ability to focus on longer-term prospects and disregard the prevailing current views. This ability to fixate on probable *future* events rather than react on the basis of *current* events creates a deep divide between successful investors and mediocre investors.

Armed with his distinct viewpoint that *incidentally* was contrary to popular opinion, Uncle John was ready to seize the opportunity to buy stocks whose prices did not reflect his views of better economic times, if not booming economic times, over the coming years. In light of the deep conviction that he developed from years of study, firsthand observation of the Nazis, the willingness of the United States to defend freedom, and the probable effects of war on industry in the context of historical precedent, he calculated a bold move: He would borrow money to purchase the shares. Here again we must pause and make a careful distinction. Uncle John had saved and already possessed all the money (and then some) he needed to buy the stocks he wanted, but he figured that in the course of business reasonable businessmen and businesswomen routinely employ debt in their business ventures.

Taken in this sense, borrowing money was not only okay but sensible. Borrowing for consumption, in contrast, was not sensible. With this in mind, he contacted his former boss, Dick Platt, at Fenner and Beane and described his thoughts and then asked to borrow $10,000 to purchase all the stocks trading below $1 on both exchanges in the United States. This may strike many as a peculiar request: In addition to choosing stocks under $1, he set out to purchase very many stocks.

Two important investment ideas can be extracted from this strategy. Moreover, when we expose them individually and give them closer consideration, they are backed by commonsense judgment. First and foremost, his fundamental thesis was that even the least efficient businesses would be revived in the economic boom stimulated by war. The companies that Uncle John targeted were pretty ordinary or even less than ordinary, were facing well-known problems, and had limited prospects (outside of an improbable economic resurgence). In other words, expectations for those companies were exceptionally low. To add to the situation, the stock market at that time had little patience for a company with limited prospects as the economy appeared to be worsening rather than improving. In effect, Uncle John ventured down into the doldrums, the literal bottom rung of the market, to purchase the stocks of those companies where sentiment was the *most* negative.

Here is the simple reason: Because he believed in a resurgence for all the businesses in the United States, even the least efficient, those stocks would demonstrate the most dramatic rises if his forecast proved correct, which he believed it would. If the market reassessed those companies' prospects as being positive, they would have the largest potential payoff by far from that reversal in sentiment and fundamentals. From a fundamental perspective, they had the potential to swing from bankruptcy to profits, or as they say, from the worst of times to the best of times. These extreme situations of negative sentiment often result in the best returns in investing. In this situation it was easy to distinguish an extreme mismatch between the values assigned to those companies by the stock market and the values that he was predicting for them when business improved in a booming war economy.

Another important lesson to be noted here was his purchase of many stocks. By purchasing many stocks instead of just a few, Uncle John was diversifying his risk. Uncle John has a deep sense and appreciation of probability, and he nearly always verbalizes his thoughts on investment in those terms. In this case his use of diversification was a rational acknowledgment that not all the investments he made would work out, and so he wanted to spread the risk of a poor investment among many stocks. In fact, of the 104 companies that Uncle John purchased in this transaction, 37 were already in bankruptcy, and so he was well aware that he needed to spread his eggs around rather than place them all in one basket.

Throughout his years as a mutual fund manager Uncle John always spoke of the benefits of diversification, and that was his practice when he managed money on behalf of others. As we will see in later chapters, however, he is hardly afraid to concentrate his investments either (even into just a few stocks), which he routinely did with his own money after retiring from managing the money of others. For instance, the meaning of the word *diversification* can change with the circumstances. While managing the Templeton Funds, Uncle John talked of owning a few hundred stocks at any particular time, and in other talks he has stated that diversification can be accomplished through simply holding no more than 10 stocks. For the time being, though, his advice is that the majority of investors benefit from diversifying their assets among various stocks. The situation in 1939 was no different, particularly since he was using borrowed money.

His timing was impeccable. As the record shows, his first investment made in accordance with the principle of maximum pessimism paid off handsomely. Just as he hypothesized, the European war led to a second world war in which America became involved, and that in turn led to a tremendous surge in demand for industrial materials, commodities, and so on, in the United States. Within a year Uncle John had repaid all the money he borrowed. Over the ensuing years he eventually sold off his holdings and turned his original $10,000 investment into $40,000, a fourfold increase. Moreover, of the 104 stocks he purchased, only 4 did not pan out. His average holding period was four years, which coincides fairly well with his average holding periods throughout his career and his tendency to forecast business conditions out five years or more.

Among his holdings in that trade, his purchase of the Missouri Pacific Railroad often is cited as particularly rewarding. The security was a preferred stock, meaning that by design it was to issue a cash dividend into perpetuity that would be paid to its holders. At its original issue price of $100, it carried a $7 dividend, or a 7 percent dividend yield. By the time Uncle John purchased the shares, the company was in bankruptcy and the preferred shares were trading at an eighth of a dollar, or about 0.125 cent per share, quite a discount from the original $100 offering price. As Uncle John's forecasts for better railway profits came to fruition, the stock eventually rose to $5, a 3,900 percent increase. To give you a sense of the fundamental turnaround that occurred at Missouri Pacific Railroad in the early 1940s, see Table 2.1, which depicts its financial performance.

Table 2.1

Missouri Pacific Railroad

	Sales ($MM)	Sales Growth, %	Net Income ($MM)	Net Income Growth, %
1939	83		−30	
1940	87	4.8	−13	56.7
1941	111	27.6	4	69.2
1942	178	60.4	31	675

As evidenced by the table, the sales and net income of Missouri Pacific increased rapidly from the point where Uncle John made his purchase. Taking this dramatic change in the company's earnings record into account, it is relatively easy to see how the stock price also rose far above the bottomed-out price of $0.125 to $5.

Another important concept here involves comparison. An important aspect of this purchase is that Missouri Pacific was certainly not the only railroad in the United States at the time or the only railroad to benefit from the improved economy that resulted from war. In fact, there were other railroads that were not on the fringes of financial performance or close to bankruptcy. A good example of a successful railroad at the time was Norfolk and Western Railway, which had strung together 50 years of earnings without losses. It might have been very tempting to purchase that fine operator because the downside risk was much lower. However, pitting the two companies against each other revealed that there was much less upside available in Norfolk and Western simply because it was well run and because of the way the government treated companies that were well run during a war boom. At the time, the government taxed the level of incremental earnings that resulted from the boom in a well-run company at a rate of 85.5

percent. In other words, a company that had been operating successfully going into the war had the "excess profits" that resulted from the war taxed at an extraordinarily high rate. Conversely, a company, such as Missouri Pacific, that had been posting losses was not subject to those taxes because it was carrying forward losses that counted against its tax bill. As a result of these somewhat peculiar tax rules, a well-run company such as Norfolk and Western stood to benefit far less from the war boom than did a weak, marginal company such as Missouri Pacific. Naturally, the same goes for the owners of the two companies. Understanding the relationship between those two companies and their respective tax treatments would have made all the difference in predicting the returns the two firms generated during the boom.

In Table 2.2, pay special attention to the growth in net income between the two companies. It is easy to see that Missouri Pacific's shareholders were getting a much better deal than were Norfolk and Western's shareholders. Take, for instance, the peak year of sales for both companies: 1942. In that year the Missouri Pacific's net income increased 675 percent whereas Norfolk and Western's declined 21.4 percent. Why did Missouri Pacific's net income surge so much higher?

Table 2.2

Comparison of Two Railroads

	Norfolk and Western		Missouri Pacific		Norfolk and Western		Missouri Pacific	
	Sales ($MM)	Sales Growth, %	Sales ($MM)	Sales Growth, %	Net Income ($MM)	Net Income Growth, %	Net Income ($MM)	Net Income Growth, %
1939	93		83		30		-30	
1940	105	12.9	87	4.8	32	6.7	-13	56.7
1941	120	14.3	111	27.6	28	-12.5	4	69.2
1942	140	16.7	178	60.4	22	-21.4	31	675

First, it had better sales growth, and second, it did not have Uncle Sam's fingers in the cookie jar, unlike Norfolk and Western. Because the government took the excess profits from Norfolk and Western through the special tax, it was effectively a bad deal. Examining these relationships demonstrates that purchasing the weaker company was a wise move in this instance. "In this instance" is the key phrase here as often it is wise to purchase a better company, all things being equal. This example is not meant to instruct bargain hunters to purchase marginal companies if they have a choice between stocks. Instead, the lesson is to be flexible in one's approach to investment selection. A bargain hunter who ignores important details such as tax treatments or is beholden to a strategy of purchasing only the best companies can miss golden opportunities in the market.

As you may have surmised from Uncle John's purchase of only marginal companies that were in or near bankruptcy, his strategy was twofold. He wanted the companies whose results would improve the most, but he also wanted to shield himself from the government taking the lion's share of the rewards. This was incredibly perceptive on his part because when he made his purchase, the United States had not entered war and the excess profit tax was not in place. However, by studying history he was well aware of this risk as the U.S. government had implemented those wartime taxes in the past. During World War I, the government had taxed the firms that were generally well run and profitable under normal circumstances. You can see that it was not enough simply to forecast a probable war and the boom that followed; it was also a matter of determining the outcome through a more careful assessment. Bargain hunters should realize the importance of history in investing. In this case, had Uncle John purchased the better companies, his results would have been far less good.

To give you an idea of what kind of difference it would have made in his investment returns, let us take a look at two baskets of companies in Table 2.3. In the first basket we have a collection of companies that posted frequent losses in the years leading up to the war, and in the other basket we have a collection of well-run companies that managed to generate earnings consistently in the years leading up to the war. In both baskets we provide the returns produced by the respective companies' stocks over the five years after 1940.

You can see from Table 2.3 that the return from the marginal companies of 1,085 percent far exceeded the return of 11 percent generated by the much better companies on the right side of the table. Despite the fact the companies on the right were well run (many are

Table 2.3

Comparison of Successful and Unsuccessful Companies

Company with Frequent Losses before 1940	Five-Year Return in Stock Price, %	Company with No Losses before 1940	Five-Year Return in Stock Price, %
Century Ribbon Mills	336	American Can	7
Colorado and Southern Railroad	3,785	Consolidated Gas Company of Baltimore	0
Crosley Corp.	724	Eastman-Kodak	30
Gotham Hosiery	900	General Foods	7
Ken-Rad Tube and Lamp	789	Great Atlantic and Pacific Tea	2
Missouri-Kansas-Texas Railroad	58	Parke-Davis	3
Reo Motor Car Company	2,033	Procter & Gamble	5
Seaboard Railroad 6-45	1,080	Timken Roller Bearing	10
Thompson-Starrett	344	Union Carbide	22
Willys-Overland	800	Hartford Fire Insurance	23
Average	**1,085**	**Average**	**11**

still around), they were not wise investments under the circumstances at that time. This should provide a good example of why it pays to know history as well as why it pays to think outside the box and look at the stocks of companies that everyone else refuses to consider.

After about four years of holding his 1939 purchases on average, Uncle John divested his trade. He sold on the fundamental premise that these companies were not as attractive after their prices had been bid so high, and the likelihood that once the war stimulus dissipated they would remain mediocre higher cost operators subject to increasing competition. Despite the tremendous coup and skyrocketing returns, Uncle John points out one of the small defeats he took in this trade: He sold a bit too early. For example, take Missouri Pacific, which he purchased for $0.125. The stock eventually rose to $105 per share over the next several years. Within the realm of errors one can make in holding and selling a stock, this one is a bit more palatable than some of the alternatives. However, it still prompted Uncle John to go back and challenge his methods of deciding when to sell a stock. Over the course of years of practice and consideration, he eventually developed a method for selling a holding successfully. We discuss his guidelines for when to sell a stock in the coming chapters.

In the meantime, we need to revisit some of the most important lessons from this chapter. First, if you are a reader of the financial press or watch any of the television programs that feature professional investors, you may encounter many negative references to volatility in the markets. As you can see from our discussions, however, volatility is your best ally in the search for bargains to purchase. Think of it this way: Volatility presents opportunities. The greater the volatility, the greater the opportunities to locate a bargain. If you are a purchaser of bargain stocks, volatility is your friend; if you are a purchaser of popular story stocks, volatility is your enemy.

Second, the biggest opportunities for a mismatch between the value of a company and its quoted stock price tend to occur when the market is obsessed with negativity. One of the easiest ways for a stock price to become too low relative to the company's worth is for it to be sold off, which drives the price down. Stocks typically are sold by investors when it has become unpopular to hold them. Stocks usually become unpopular because the company has run into problems, which have become publicized in the market. As a bargain hunter, you must become accustomed to sizing up these problems and assessing their impact on the ongoing business.

The truth is that all companies face problems; some are better known than others, and some are more serious than others. Problems for a company that appear to be temporary often represent the best situations to invest in as myopic holders of the stock get upset by a change in near-term expectations. It is very important to think of a company as an entity that will operate as long as it can sustain itself and make profits for its owners above its cost of capital. If you have this perspective and are confident in the lifelong prospects of the business, it becomes easier to purchase stocks that are sold off because of a poor quarterly earnings result. These events happen all the time and create opportunities for those with patience. Put another way, Michael Jordan, arguably the greatest basketball player ever, had a few bad nights, missed a few game-winning shots here and there, and so on. It clearly would have been a mistake to dump him from the Chicago Bulls because of a bad game or two over the span of such a stellar career.

Finally, your potential returns as a bargain hunter can scale conversely with the amount of pessimism that has gripped the stock price. In other words, when the views of the market become most pessimistic on a company, your potential to make money by holding the stock scales proportionately if there is a reversal in sentiment or prospects for the company. The worse the outlook, the greater the reward if that outlook changes. This is the basic premise behind investing at the point of maximum pessimism: When the mood surrounding the stock changes, you stand to generate the most exceptional returns available in the stock price. Another way to think about this is to look for stocks when the market has become extremely unreasonable and take advantage of that unreasonable view. Adopting this mindset can be counterintuitive because as humans we are always looking for the best prospects available in all of our endeavors. As a bargain hunter you must search for pessimism in areas where the situation causing the negative outlook is temporary.

Do not take it from us, though. In Uncle John's words, "People are always asking me where the outlook is good, but that's the wrong question. The right question is: Where is the outlook most miserable?"

Chapter | 3

THE UNCOMMON COMMON SENSE OF GLOBAL INVESTING

It seems to be common sense that if you are going to search for these unusually good bargains, you wouldn't just search in Canada. If you search just in Canada, you will find some, or if you search just in the United States, you will find some. But why not search everywhere? That's what we've been doing for forty years; we search anywhere in the world.

— Sir John Templeton, November 1979

The idea of global investing has become more mainstream. There are many mutual funds that offer investors a chance to compound their savings in the various stock markets outside the United States. Despite the broad acceptance of global investing today, for many decades foreign markets were underexploited and largely misunderstood. For lack of better words, investing overseas used to be a foreign concept.

When Uncle John launched the Templeton Growth Fund in November 1954, he was on the cutting edge of global investing. Often referred to as the "Dean of Global Investing" by *Forbes* magazine, Uncle John never had a problem looking past geographical borders to find a bargain stock to purchase. There are two commonsense reasons for leaving the domestic market behind to find bargain stocks. The first is to widen and deepen the pool of possible bargains. If your goal as a bargain hunter is to purchase only the stocks that offer the largest differential between the stock market price and your calculation of what a business is worth, searching worldwide for these bargains makes sense. For one thing, the bargain inventory from which to choose is exponentially larger. For instance, your inventory for selection may jump from approximately 3,000 stocks in the United States to approximately 20,000 worldwide. Therefore, your chances to succeed over the long-haul are much higher if you stay flexible and let the various stock markets around the world tell you where to invest.

In addition to obtaining a wider selection to choose from, it is common to find relatively better bargains in one country than in another. If your mission is to exploit the opportunities created by pessimism, fear, or negativity, it is likely that one country will have a better outlook than another. The differing outlooks and sentiment surrounding the various countries creates asymmetry in the pricing of the assets in one country versus another. Put more simply, differing outlooks may make stocks a better bargain in one country than in another. As a bargain hunter you want to maximize the asymmetry between a stock price and the company's estimated value. Therefore, if asymmetry shows up in one particular country, it may represent a collection of bargains. In contrast, if the risk is too much to bear, it may not. Judging these risks is an important step and one that we discuss later in this chapter.

Just as important, if you seek the best bargains available regardless of where they are located, you gain the added benefit of diversification. History has provided many examples of times when it was a bad idea to have all one's investments tied up in the United States, in any single country, or in any single asset class for that matter. It is futile to try to make a combined guess about what will pay off and when. Expanding on this line of reasoning, diversification is a good way to protect you from *yourself*. The simple truth is that no one has ever been successful at picking which market will perform *and* when. Diversification is also generally a good policy because in many of your investment selections as a bargain hunter, you will spot opportunities before others and therefore invest sooner than others do. This is a very common trait in bargain hunting and value investors.

Often your near-term prize for spotting bargains ahead of the crowd is to sit around and wait for the market's attitudes or perceptions to improve. Sometimes the wait can last several years. Just as often, bargain hunters purchase a stock that continues to fall in price. Therefore, patience is not only a virtue, it is a key characteristic of successful value investors. In light of the common circumstance of a lengthy waiting period, there is a benefit to having your investments spread around: When sentiment changes, it changes very quickly. If you wait for sentiment to change before you invest, guess what? You are following the crowd. Also and most important, you have missed out on a big portion, if not all, of the returns generated by the change in sentiment. Uncle John always said that when sentiment changes, it changes very suddenly, and if you are not invested, you will miss out on a large proportion of the returns. These initial returns may be enough by themselves to separate you from the average returns of the market. If you are following the crowd, you will achieve the same results the crowd achieves. Furthermore, years of research show that the crowd's results are pretty disappointing, often falling short of the index averages. In either case, diversifying your assets across more than one country will tend to water down any singular pain from a long wait or from being wrong altogether. Moreover, it is not unusual to see some of your holdings appreciating out of sync with the remainder of your portfolio. Uncle John's advice on the benefits of diversification is that "the only investors who shouldn't diversify are those who are right 100 percent of the time."

For anyone who remains skeptical about the benefits of diversification, we offer Figure 3.1 (see pages 60–61). It is what is known as a "periodic table of investment returns," and we have included it to demonstrate the rotation of the world's various markets performance from good to bad and vice versa.

As Figure 3.1 shows, hitching a cart to only one horse in the market can lead to underperformance for years at a time. In contrast, having your assets a bit more spread out leads to better and more balanced results. A good way to perceive this relationship among the various markets around the world is to think in terms of opportunity cost. Opportunity cost is a popular concept in both economics and finance that states that with every action we take, we give up the benefits of taking an alternative action. In this context, the opportunity cost of investing only in the United States (assuming we can achieve the results of the S&P 500) can be very high. For instance, in 2002 your funds would have returned –22.1 percent if they had been invested only in the S&P 500, and that assumes that you achieved a return as good as that of the S&P 500. Conversely, if you had spread your money evenly throughout these markets, you would have generated a return of –14.5 percent. For many of you, losing less money may seem to be nothing to crow about, but if you are saving for retirement or your children's education, avoiding losses can make a large difference over time. Think about it this way: If you were invested only in the S&P 500 in 2002, you gave up making an extra 10 percent on your money. This exercise is illuminating, but it is always more helpful to view ideas at work in the real world.

Let's consider a real-world example that illustrates the benefits of combining diversification and bargain hunting into one strategy. In this example, we will look at a real money manager investing real money and making real people wealthy for a nearly 40-year period. This example, shown in Figure 3.2 on page 62, examines one of the best investment vehicles we know: the Templeton Growth Fund. Uncle John managed the Templeton Growth Fund from 1954 to 1987.

As the figure shows, if you had been fortunate enough to invest $10,000 in the Templeton Growth Fund at its inception in 1954, you would have seen your original investment increase to over $2 million by the time Uncle John sold his funds to Franklin Resources in 1992. This fund was operated on the basic premises of bargain hunting that we described in Chapter 2 as well as the introductory material on global investing in this chapter. In other words, the growth of the $10,000 investment shown in the figure was the result of searching for and investing in the best bargains available in the market regardless of geography. One purpose of this illustration is to demonstrate the benefits of diversification empirically.

Of course, you could have played it safe and invested only in the U.S. market over that period. However, your account would have accumulated only $100,935 if it had been invested in the S&P 500. Applying the concept of opportunity cost, you would have forgone the extra $1.9 million earned in the Templeton Growth Fund from the

Figure 3.1

Periodic Table of Investment Returns

1993	1994	1995	1996	1997	1998	1999
Hong Kong 116.7%	Japan 21.4%	S&P 500 37.6%	Hong Kong 33.1%	S&P 500 33.4%	Germany 29.4%	MSCI EM 66.9%
MSCI EM 74.8%	MSCI EAFE 7.8%	Russell 2000 28.5%	UK 27.4%	Germany 24.6%	S&P 500 28.6%	Japan 61.5%
Germany 35.6%	Germany 4.7%	Hong Kong 22.6%	S&P 500 23.0%	UK 22.6%	MSCI EAFE 20.0%	Hong Kong 59.5%
MSCI EAFE 32.6%	S&P 500 1.3%	UK 21.3%	Russell 2000 16.5%	Russell 2000 22.4%	UK 17.8%	MSCI EAFE 30.0%
Japan 25.5%	UK −1.6%	LB Agg 18.5%	Germany 13.6%	LB Agg 9.7%	LB Agg 8.7%	Russell 2000 21.3%
UK 24.4%	Russell 2000 −1.8%	Germany 16.4%	MSCI EAFE 6.1%	MSCI EAFE 1.8%	Japan 5.1%	S&P 500 21.0%
Russell 2000 18.9%	LB Agg −2.9%	MSCI EAFE 11.2%	MSCI EM 6.0%	MSCI EM −11.6%	Russell 2000 −2.6%	Germany 20.0%
S&P 500 10.1%	MSCI EM −7.3%	Japan 0.7%	LB Agg 3.6%	Hong Kong −23.3%	Hong Kong −2.9%	UK 12.5%
LB Agg 9.8%	Hong Kong −28.9%	MSCI EM −5.2%	Japan −15.5%	Japan −23.7%	MSCI EM −25.4%	LB Agg −0.8%

Key:

LB Agg = Lehman Brothers Aggregate Bond Index
MSCI EM = Morgan Stanley Capital International Emerging Market Index
MSCI EAFE = Morgan Stanley Capital International Europe, Australasia, Far East Index
Hong Kong, Germany, Japan, UK = Morgan Stanley Capital International Individual Country Indices
Russell 2000 = 2,000 smallest companies in the Russell 3,000 Index
S&P 500 = Standard and Poor's capitalization weighted Index of 500 stocks representing all major Industries

Source: Bloomberg

2000	2001	2002	2003	2004	2005	2006
LB Agg 11.6%	LB Agg 8.4%	LB Agg 10.3%	Germany 63.8%	MSCI EM 25.9%	MSCI EM 34.5%	Germany 36.0%
Russell 2000 −3.0%	Russell 2000 2.5%	MSCI EM −6.0%	MSCI EM 56.3%	Hong Kong 25.0%	Japan 25.5%	MSCI EM 32.6%
S&P 500 −9.1%	MSCI EM −2.4%	Japan −10.3%	Russell 2000 47.3%	MSCI EAFE 20.3%	MSCI EAFE 13.5%	UK 30.6%
UK −11.5%	S&P 500 −11.9%	UK −15.2%	MSCI EAFE 35.6%	UK 19.6%	Germany 9.9%	Hong Kong 30.4%
MSCI EAFE −14.2	UK −14.1%	MSCI EAFE −15.9%	Hong Kong 38.1%	Russell 2000 15.3%	Hong Kong 8.4%	MSCI EAFE 26.3%
Hong Kong −14.7%	Hong Kong −15.6%	Hong Kong −17.3%	Japan 35.9%	Germany 16.2%	UK 7.4%	Russell 2000 18.4%
Germany −15.6%	MSCI EAFE −21.4%	Russell 2000 −20.5%	UK 32.1%	Japan 15.9%	S&P 500 4.9%	S&P 500 15.8%
Japan −28.2%	Germany −22.4%	S&P 500 −22.1%	S&P 500 25.7%	S&P 500 10.9%	Russell 2000 4.6%	Japan 6.2%
MSCI EM −30.7%	Japan −29.4%	Germany −33.2%	LB Agg 4.1%	LB Agg 4.3%	LB Agg 2.4%	LB Agg 4.3%

Figure 3.2

Returns from the Templeton Growth Fund and the S&P 500, 1955–1992

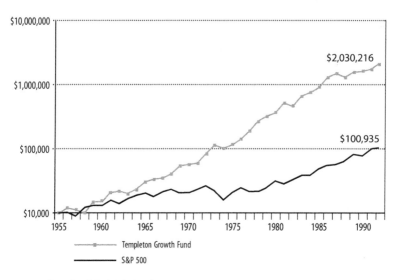

Sources: Templeton Growth Fund, Ltd.; Bloomberg

original $10,000. In this context, we can see that limiting your investing to the United States is an expensive habit, one that carries a seven-figure price tag in this case. There are not too many sensible people who would refuse an extra $1.9 million in their brokerage accounts over the life of their investments. However, investors who did not invest in the global markets with Uncle John in 1954 gave up $1.9 million for every $10,000 they invested in the S&P 500.

Although the growth of a $10,000 investment in the Templeton Growth Fund may persuade some people that global diversification is advantageous, what about those who question our strategy of purchasing only the best bargains in the market? Perhaps some investors may be sold on diversification but are averse to the idea of buying the stocks of companies that are out of favor, boring, despised, uninspiring, or simply unknown to the masses. We will demonstrate that it pays to be a bargain hunter in addition to diversifying through global investments.

Although a good global benchmark is not available going all the way back to 1954, the widely known MSCI World Index posts data from 1969 forward. Figure 3.3 examines the advantages of bargain hunting on a global basis versus investing on a global basis in a broad index such as the MSCI World Index.

As we consider the results of $10,000 invested in the Templeton Growth Fund versus $10,000 invested in a broad index such as the MSCI World, the disparity in performance is again meaningful. If we had invested the $10,000 in the Templeton Growth Fund in 1969, we would have accumulated $363,949 by 1992 (assuming that we rein-

Figure 3.3

Value of $10,000 Invested in Templeton Growth Fund and MSCI World Index, 1970–1992

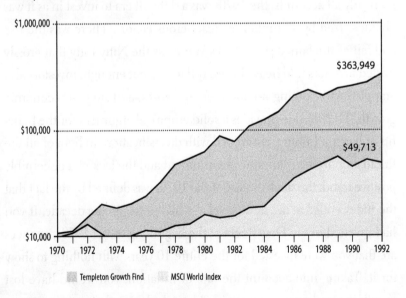

Templeton Growth Find   MSCI World Index

Sources: Templeton Growth Fund, Ltd.; Bloomberg

vested distributions and dividends). If we simply had invested in the stocks represented by the MSCI World Index, we would have seen our assets grow to $49,713. Importantly, investors have to ask themselves what they give up by not adapting a bargain-hunting selection process or placing their investments with practitioners who apply those methods. The answer in the case of Uncle John's fund was simple: You volunteered to forfeit an additional $314,236 of your wealth. Of course, this assumes you can pick stocks like Uncle John or create returns above the index known as alpha. When we look at the case for investing as a bargain hunter on a global basis in this light, the question is not whether you should search the world for bargains. The real question is, can you afford not to? If the answer is a commonsense no, you are well on your way to gaining the perspective of a global bargain hunter.

What may be overlooked by some as they glance at Figure 3.3 is the strong performance of the Templeton Growth Fund during the 1970s. By nearly all accounts, the 1970s was a difficult era to invest in as it was characterized by a number of treacherous factors. There was the rise and fall of the famed story stocks known as the Nifty Fifty that grossly misled investors into heavy losses. If that was not enough, investors also grappled with surging inflation, energy crises, and sluggish economic growth. That decade provides a solid empirical argument for the benefits of bargain hunting combined with diversification. In light of all the fluctuation in the economic environment and the lack of a discernibly positive trend, the stock market of the 1970s was defined by the fact that the index ended at the same level at which it began the decade. If you had invested in the Dow stocks at the beginning of the 1970s, chances are that you were invested for the entire 10 years with nothing to show for it. Taking into account the rate of inflation, you would have lost wealth as purchasing power eroded heavily during that time.

Figure 3.4

The Dow Jones Industrial Average, 1969–1979

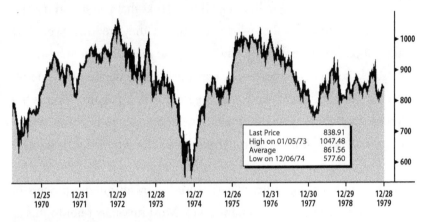

Last Price	838.91
High on 01/05/73	1047.48
Average	861.56
Low on 12/06/74	577.60

Source: Bloomberg

Figure 3.4 shows the U.S. market over that period and provides an opportunity to raise an important question: Does the stock market have to go up for you to make money? The simple answer is no. If you are executing your strategy as a bargain hunter correctly—purchasing only the stocks that are lowest in relation to your estimation of their companies' worth—you effectively are investing in only the best opportunities available. In using this method, you are not necessarily tagging along with the performance of the market unless, coincidentally, the stocks that have the lowest price in relation to their worth happen to be in one of the popular market proxies, such as the Dow Jones Industrial Average, the S&P 500, or the NASDAQ. This has happened before, for example, in the early 1980s, when Uncle John loaded up on the "famous name stocks" in the United States as their P/E ratios had become thoroughly depressed to less than half their long-term averages. More often than not, though, your collection of stocks will be unknown to most or avoided by most. The broader idea at work here is to piece together on a stock-by-stock basis your most attractive collection of bargains available in the market.

When you are done collecting all the stocks that you found trading at less than perhaps half of what you estimate they are worth, you may take a look at your collection and conclude that the large majority of the stocks trade in one particular country, such as Japan. At this point, you may be inclined to say, "Japanese stocks are a bargain." This is the process that guides you into making what appears to be a macroeconomic call on a country. Throughout his career, Uncle John was well known for his ability to choose a country to invest in, but few realize that his views on a country always were led by an intense process of examining stocks at the company level. Most investors refer to this as a "bottom-up" analysis. That is, you start at the bottom level of the market—the individual company—when you look for investments. This is one area where Uncle John probably was misunderstood. Many observers assume that because he usually recommends one country versus another, he's been sizing up the two countries at a macroeconomic level to make his decision. More often, however, he has concluded that a country is a good investment by first locating a concentration of cheap stocks that happen to be in one country versus another. In other words, his country views are the result of an assimilation of bottom-up analysis rather than starting with some view of the top-down level on the country's GDP, outlook for employment, or the like. Bargain hunters should realize that getting a country right begins with getting individual companies right, not the other way around.

The appropriate way to look at the "stock market" is to view it as a collection of stocks rather than an index number. When you view the market on a stock-by-stock basis, you will find that at any particular time the stock market contains a number of individual bull markets and bear markets. In fact, each stock is its own stock market; that is, each stock is composed of a number of buyers and sellers. In applying this perspective, it is possible to locate a number of stocks that could perform well during a bear market for the indexes or poorly during a bull market for the indexes.

Sometimes the effect of this type of analysis is to disconnect your performance from that of the broader market indexes such as the Dow Jones, S&P 500, and MSCI World Index. This sounds great and truly is great when your bargain stocks are rising in price and the index is falling. The flip side is that you may have stretches where your holdings perform worse than the market averages. This is a psychological form of indigestion that few investors, even experienced ones, can stomach with ease, but it is a common backdrop to successful investing over the long term. History shows that although your overall performance as an investor may be superior to the market averages, you can expect periods in which your performance falls short of the market. Sometimes you may underperform by a wide margin. Your edge as a bargain hunter is to have conviction that you did your homework up front and that time is on your side. The market eventually will recognize what you already know. A few years of underperformance compared to the market should be *expected*.

If you accept this basic reality at the outset, you will have the psychological strength not to cut and run when the ball does not bounce your way in the short term. The urge to switch out of your losing investments and into "better" investments — usually meaning something that is rising in price — may be overwhelming. It is important to resist these urges if your original analysis and research are sound. No matter whose track record you are examining among the great mutual fund investors who have been at it for a decade or more, you will see that they went through periods of underperformance in spite of their long-term ability to outperform the market.

Figure 3.5

Annual Returns of Templeton Growth Fund and Dow Jones Industrial Average, 1970–1979

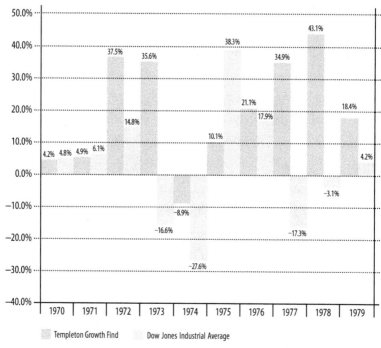

Templeton Growth Fund Ltd.; Bloomberg

A good example of the consequences of getting unnerved by near-term underperformance can be seen in Figure 3.5, which shows the annual returns of the Templeton Growth Fund and the Dow Jones Industrial Average. For investors who were disturbed by the fund's underperformance in 1970, 1971, or 1975, it would have been a big mistake to sell shares because the fund compounded a return of 22 percent in the decade compared with 4.6 percent for the Dow. However, investors from all backgrounds, whether bargain hunters for stocks or bargain hunters for mutual funds, typically play musical chairs at the worst possible time because of near-term underperformance. Recognizing this psychological handicap to investing led Uncle John to offer the following advice: "The time to reflect on your investing methods is when you are most successful, not when you are making the most mistakes."

Up to this point we have presented some real-life empirical arguments for bargain hunting on a global basis. However, even in this day and age, there are investors who ignore the global markets and continue to invest only in the United States. The current views are only slightly less ridiculous than the views that were prevalent among his classmates when Uncle John studied at Yale in the 1930s. Back then the consensus was that the United States was the most important country and therefore the best market for investment. Now the usual complaint is that investing overseas entails a general lack of information. To complicate the issue, the naysayers have this one right! It is generally true that there is less information available on foreign companies, particularly if you are looking to invest in emerging markets. However, your perspective on this reality can help seal your fate as a global bargain hunter. Do you see the glass half empty? Are you scared off by the lack of information? Or do you see the glass as half full? Can you *take advantage* of this lack of information and seize it as an opportunity to make an investment ahead of the crowd? Uncle John is the eternal optimist, and his practical response is to roll up his sleeves and do his homework. Bargain hunters need to realize that finding stocks about which information is lacking is an effective way to find mispricings.

A good example of these information gaps and a working example of how Uncle John tackled them comes from his purchase of the Mexican telephone company Telefonos de Mexico in the mid-1980s. At that time, the company's reported numbers were unreliable in Uncle John's opinion. His solution was to count the number of telephones in that country and multiply that number by the rate the citizens were paying. This required a great deal of work and research, but he then was able to determine that the stock price was far too low compared with what the company was worth, using his own projections. This example may sound a bit extreme, but it is a good illustration of what a bargain hunter must be prepared to do in searching for the truth.

This discussion should begin to sound eerily familiar after our talks in Chapter 2 about the market's perceptions and how they can become detached from the economic reality that governs the worth of a business. Misperception of a stock and its relation to its company can come in many forms, and lack of information is a great source of misperception in the global markets and in the emerging markets in particular. In the case of the telephone company, the lack of information kept investors away. Because investors avoided the stock for this reason, it was only common sense to investigate the situation and look for the truth, since investors had driven the price down from a simple lack of knowledge about the company. Investors' unwillingness to dig and get the right information created an opportunity that Uncle John exploited.

Often, the only hurdle is your unwillingness to work just a bit harder than the next guy or gal to get the answers. Uncle John always considers this intense work ethic as a basic philosophy underlying success, whether in investing or in any other pursuit. This belief in an exponential payoff to working harder than the next person is what he refers to as the "doctrine of the extra ounce." This is akin to a famous piece of advice once offered by Henry Ford: "Genius is 1 percent inspiration and 99 percent perspiration." Uncle John believes that in all walks of life, those who became moderately successful did *almost* as much work as those who were the *most* successful. In other words, what separates the best from all the rest is a willingness to put in that one extra hour of reading, that one extra hour of conditioning, that one extra hour of training, that one extra hour of study. Everyone has run across someone who was loaded with natural talent in his or her profession, sport, or classroom but never generated the amount of success that was there for the taking. This reveals that sometimes being the brightest student or the most gifted athlete is a handicap. This is true in every walk of life and every pursuit, not just investing. The best bargain hunters realize that the one extra annual report they read, the one extra competing company they interview, or the one extra newspaper article they scan may be the tipping point for the best investment they ever make.

Over the last 30 years or so the growth in global investing has produced more and more analysts looking at securities, and that has led to an increase in published research. This growth in global investors and the various brokerages that service them with research has eroded some of the more glaring inefficiencies in the market. However, we have found that the market is still teeming with stocks that have no research coverage or only a few analysts covering them. These stocks should be considered a prime hunting ground for bargain hunters who are willing to put in the work and do some original bottom-up analysis. Stocks in the foreign markets with very little research coverage can carry major inefficiencies involving what is occurring in their businesses and how the market perceives those businesses. Looking for and spotting these mismatches is a tried-and-true technique for successful global bargain hunting.

With all this talk about searching worldwide for bargain stocks and exploiting the inefficiencies created in the market by a lack of information, we have not discussed the guiding light that leads the bargain hunter into a proposed purchase. For Uncle John the guiding light most often has been the P/E ratio. This may strike some as very simplistic, but the truth is that the P/E ratio (price divided by earnings per share) is a good proxy or *starting* point for valuation. Low P/Es led Uncle John into Japan in the 1960s, the United States in the 1980s, and South Korea in the late 1990s. All three of those "country calls" proved to be exceptional investments. Of course, we do not suggest that you scoop up every stock with a low P/E you can get your hands on, but one of his basic premises is to pay as little as possible for future earnings.

To tilt the probabilities of success in your favor, you should search for a stock priced exceptionally low relative to the earnings of a company that has better than average *long-term* growth prospects and better than average *long-term* earnings power. Your best chances of executing this strategy most likely will occur in stocks that have been sold off and are out of favor, unknown to wider audiences, or misunderstood by the market. To give you some idea of what his benchmarks of value were, Uncle John often looked for stocks that were trading at no more than five times the current share price divided by his estimate of earnings five years into the future. In other words, his calculation of the company's earnings per share in year 5 divided into the stock price was less than or equal to the number 5. Likewise, he has remarked that occasionally he was able to pay only one to two times his estimate of earnings to be reported in the coming year. That, of course, is dealing in an extreme situation of depressed value. However, this is exactly what bargain hunters must be on the lookout for: *extreme* cases of mispricing.

You may ask, how can anyone be certain about what a company will earn five years down the road? Well, few people can with any precision. Most analysts tackle this question by forecasting a reversion to the average historical results of the company, provided that no substantial changes appear to be on the horizon for the company or its industry. Put another way, if the long-term average net profit margin over the last 10 years is 5 percent but the company has made 7 percent in the last year, the bargain hunter may be wise to use a 5 percent margin over the coming five years unless, of course, the company has accomplished something that will alter its earning power permanently and it is therefore reasonable to expect 7 percent to be the norm going forward. A conservative bargain hunter may forecast with the 5 percent margin, just in case, as the future is uncertain after all.

This method of applying conservative assumptions in one's forecast creates a "margin of safety." The margin of safety is a concept developed by Benjamin Graham that represents a bread-and-butter staple in bargain hunting. One way to apply the basic concept is to utilize assumptions in one's projections that allow for less than ideal circumstances. The idea is to forecast the results for an entire "cycle," normally about five years, in which a bargain hunter contemplates good times as well as not so good times. Long-term bargain hunters know they must consider both scenarios. If the stock price is still low relative to these less than ideal or average results, you have located a stock with a margin of safety.

Using a medium- to longer-term five-year projection may not be the easiest task, but it forces you into a virtuous line of thinking that focuses your thoughts, questions, and discussion on topics that are more relevant to the business. For instance, what kind of competitive advantages does this company possess? If they are going to maintain their earnings power over a long period, there should be a competitive advantage for the company. Do they have a lower cost of production?

Do they have a better brand and therefore command higher selling prices as a result of a perception of quality? If the answer to any of these questions is yes, you may be more comfortable forecasting that their profit margins will be sustainable in the future. If so, this gives you a better basis to judge the company's future earnings. The simple truth is that if you are going to take a shot at projecting the future, you will need to have a more dynamic understanding of the company and its prospects. The way you obtain a dynamic understanding of a company is to ask questions about its long-term prospects. Long-term prospects are measured in years, not quarters. All the questions and answers that you will generate in your attempt to calculate earnings well into the future will provide you with a superior perspective on the company relative to the other buyers and sellers in the market.

Another important edge that accompanies looking at earnings five years down the road is that it should force you psychologically to tune out any near-term noise that has taken hold of the market. This goes back to our discussion in Chapter 2 of taking advantage of near-term volatilities created by quick movements in a stock price caused by temporary setbacks at a company. Taking a long-term view of a company is not a fanciful idea or marketing phrase used by fund managers in their advertising. When practiced correctly, it represents a psychological edge that good bargain hunters use to take advantage of temporary problems in a business.

Up to this point we have presented several arguments for the benefits of global bargain hunting, but astute investors know that bargain hunting comes with risks. The presence of those risks and a reluctance to take on some of the exposures to them keep many "global investors" with just a big toe dipped in the foreign markets, usually through one of the larger market cap companies that are "safer." Understanding and measuring the risks that come with investing around the world represents a legitimate challenge. One of the primary concerns that most investors must tackle is the issue of buying a stock and then accepting the incumbent risks that accompany its local currency.

Uncle John's advice on currency was grounded in his belief in the concept that currency trends tend to last for years. Furthermore, his view on the merits of one currency versus another was to gravitate toward the one that is "less risky" versus the one that is supposed to be "good." In other words, all currencies come with risks, but the one risk that Uncle John always seemed unwilling to take was excess spending by a government. From the earlier chapters we know that one of his basic life philosophies is to practice thrift and saving. In many ways this belief extends up the ladder to a country level. In other words, countries with modest borrowing and high savings rates have the currencies that are the least risky. The list of countries that meet this criterion has been shrinking over time, but there are still plenty around. One of the paradoxes of investing in an increasingly freer world on the heels of advancing democracy is a basic secular increase in inflation. This is not meant to imply that Uncle John does not favor democracy and free enterprise. He does support it, and with his own money. Free enterprise is one of his core philanthropic areas, in addition to progress in spirituality and character development. However, one of the trends that accompany the spread of democracy is inflation that is caused by the tendency of voters to elect officials who spend increasing amounts of money and do not save. Uncle John believes that voters always prefer more spending and will not reelect politicians who do not give them what they want. This has always been the case in democracies, and the United States is a poster child for spending. The problem is that the heavy spending can lead to excess borrowing that eventually weakens the currency of the borrowers until it reaches the point of losing value. There are extreme cases of these instances that should be studied by bargain hunters, including the defaults in the countries that were part of the Asian financial crisis (1997–1998) and Argentina (2001).

Now we are armed with a concept of what to avoid, that is, excess borrowing by a government. We should take the opportunity to translate this notion into more tangible guidelines that we can apply as bargain hunters. Uncle John provided us years ago with a basic recipe for identifying countries that should pose less risk to investors who are exposed to their currencies. First, if you want to avoid companies operating in riskier currencies, focus on companies with over 25 percent of their business performed in countries that export more goods than they import. From another perspective this means that the exporter is accumulating reserves, or savings, and the purchase of its goods from other nations also can create upward pressure on the exporter's currency (which thus should stabilize or even increase in value). The second thing to determine is that the country does not have government debts that exceed 25 percent of its annual gross national product. This measure gives bargain hunters a benchmark for what a conservatively managed government balance sheet should look like. The problem that heavily indebted countries run into occurs when creditors or investors fear that they will not be repaid or will be repaid with a currency that has been devalued. When creditors and investors become worried for these reasons, the flight from debt or investments they hold in the heavily indebted nation creates selling in that country's currency, and the selling causes it to lose value.

Another basket of risks for bargain hunters to consider relates to the political landscape of a country they are considering for investment.

As we mentioned above, Uncle John is a huge proponent of free enterprise and the freedom of individuals to pursue their interests. His
beliefs on free enterprise were formed as a young man when he read
Adam Smith's *An Inquiry into the Nature and Causes of the Wealth of
Nations*, which he considers one of the most important books ever
written. The impact of that book on his disposition was meaningful.

Uncle John always favors investing in environments where there is
less regulation and an increased ability for individuals to pursue their
goals. His belief regarding investment decisions is that if left alone,
the markets will regulate themselves to a large extent. However, in the
real world governments have a strong tendency to get involved, med-
dle, intervene, and overextend their role in business. Therefore, from
a governmental or a policy standpoint, Uncle John looked for governments that were trending toward capitalism and free markets. He
avoided countries where the practice and policies were trending
toward socialism.

A good example of this viewpoint in the current real world is that
on a stated level, China is a "communist" country. However, in practice, over the last 28 years or so the government and its markets
increasingly have been opened and the *trend* has been toward freer
markets and capitalism. In contrast to China is Venezuela, which is a
"democracy" whose president has used his authority to nationalize
assets and transfer ownership from private to public hands. This government is trending rapidly toward socialism. Socialistic trends can
present bad situations for investors, particularly if the company they
hold stock in is having its assets seized and confiscated by the government. The consequences of nationalized assets are often chronic
underinvestment of outside capital and public capital, followed by the
eventual underutilization and underperformance of the nationalized

assets. As a bargain hunter, you should avoid these situations at all costs.

Uncle John believes that ultimately you must leave people to their own devices and allow them to pursue their economic goals in an unfettered manner. This notion of leaving the markets alone was popularized by Adam Smith as laissez-faire, or hands-off. The underlying belief is that an "invisible hand" will guide the overall results to positive ground as capitalists allocate resources to the best opportunities and avoid the worst. In contrast to the invisible hand is what we could call a forcible hand utilized by a government. In a centrally planned government or socialist government, the hand that guides the market is the government.

One of the most regrettable economic actions employed by a forcible hand is transferring ownership away from individuals and into the hands of public entities controlled by the government. This action is antithetical to the system of free enterprise. Moreover, the lack of competition that results from nationalizing an industry usually creates an environment where lethargy and complacency dominate the mindset, and this in turn leads to mediocre performance. As soon as ownership is transferred, the remaining operators lose their sense of having a stake in the assets or the activity of the assets. They sense that the conventional risk of failure ending in bankruptcy is low, and this mentality can set an enterprise back years or even decades compared with free enterprise–based competition, in which companies must improve constantly or be forced out of the market. Therefore, nationalizing assets not only represents a poor investment but also goes against a deep philosophical belief that Uncle John holds. That belief is that free enterprise and the competition that results from it lead to progress. Progress is a very good and necessary thing for businesses. Progress is also a very good and necessary thing in all walks of life, whether technology, science, or any other discipline. When competition is stifled, progress is too.

Up to now we have covered the strategy of seeking bargains on a case-by-case basis as well as some of the common risks to avoid in choosing bargains from among many different countries. The necessary step after taking these two strategic components into account is to assimilate them into one view. Put another way, once you have detected your potential bargains from your bottom-up analysis, you will need to run them up the flagpole and see if you can bear the top-down country risks that accompany the investment. In some instances you may find that a company's stock price may be 50 percent or less than what you believe that company is worth. Upon further investigation, you may discover that the government that oversees the company's area of operations has implemented price controls on the company's products, not allowing the company to increase its prices. In this case, you probably would be inclined to say no to the purchase of the stock and go look for a bargain that carries a more palatable set of risks.

The basic idea here is that when you locate bargain stock ideas, you need to make an honest attempt to find out why they are mispriced. If they are mispriced because of near-term or temporary issues, the discount that is priced into the stocks should be more acceptable to bear. Of course, it is very common for a stock to be mispriced versus its longer-term value for reasons that have nothing to do with the country in which it operates. With that said, the goal is to interpret each individual situation on its own. In doing so you may begin to see patterns form that suggest that a group of stocks are underpriced because of a common factor, such as concerns about the macroeconomic environment in the country. For instance, you may find that a large group of stocks in one country are priced too low because of something that upset investors in the past, such as the prospect of slowing growth or even a real recession, but will not be the case going forward. When the reason a stock becomes a bargain is temporary, the bargain hunter should always invest.

Chapter | 4

THE FIRST TO SPOT THE RISING SUN

It is a joy to visit Japan and see the attitude of the people. Fifty or sixty years ago in the United States businessmen were admired. People took pride in working hard and producing good products. People worked on Saturdays. People were proud of the company they worked for. And all those things still exist in Japan, so Japan is going to continue to grow industrially twice as fast as the United States.
—Sir John Templeton, September 1981

By the time Uncle John made those remarks on Japan in *The Wall Street Transcript*, his funds were largely unwound from their heavy concentration in Japanese stocks as a result of their increasing popularity and rising market values. However, the quote is illuminating because it provides an important example of how he meshes his analysis of individual companies and their fair value appraisals with other considerations he believes are important. There is no question that his heavy investment in Japan was led principally by the demonstrably low P/E ratios and high growth rates that the stocks and their companies carried in the 1950s and 1960s, but his intention to sit tight in the holdings and wait for their market values to rise no doubt was driven by viewing firsthand the same qualities that he held in such high esteem: thrift, focused determination, and hard work. The people of Japan embodied those ideals, and the companies that employed them became economic manifestations of those characteristics.

During the 1980s most Americans came to the realization that Japan was a dominant economic force in the world. However, this is very far from the perceptions that Americans had of Japan in the first two decades after the end of World War II. What makes this changing belief system so remarkable is that Uncle John identified Japan as a solid investment in the 1950s, shortly after the end of the war. The world's view of Japan 30 years before the 1980s, when Uncle John started investing in that country, was hardly one of fear or admiration. By and large Japan was dismissed as a low-wage manufacturer of inferior cheap products. It was an industrial backwater in the eyes of investors in the United States. Aside from some occasional complaints about dumping practices in the textile trade, its role as a free nation in a region trending toward communism was far more important to the United States than any other consideration.

Despite that perception of economic inferiority in the United States, those careful enough to observe its actions more closely were given ample notice that it had significant ambitions to restore itself as a powerful *industrial* nation rather than a producer of low-cost trinkets. In fact, the Japanese were taking aggressive measures to study and improve their manufacturing practices and become knowledgeable about U.S. selling practices and the preferences of U.S. consumers. In 1950, when Japan opened an overseas trading agency in several U.S. locations, including New York, a Japanese government official had this to say in an article in the *New York Times*: "Other objectives of the agency will be the elimination of complaints by the American buyers about trade policies of Japanese businessmen, and the overcoming of the American public's belief that Japanese goods are 'cheap stuff.'"

Some six years later, in 1956, Japan's hard work, thrift, and focus were beginning to pay off, and the country was climbing steadily up the value chain from a producer of trinkets to a producer of technical, more complex industrial machinery. Reporters in a 1956 article in the *New York Times* were relaying this information back to the United States, but of course it was falling on deaf ears. "Where once Japan concentrated on cheap, inferior consumer goods and low priced textiles, she is now going in for machinery and quality products. . . . So Japan is placing her dependence on heavy equipment and machinery, areas in which she can compete with the United States, Britain and Europe for the Asian market." Some four years later Japan was beginning to hit its stride in the realization of its postwar goal of becoming an industrial power.

By the time 1960 rolled around, few observers in the United States were taking notice of Japan's advancing industrialism. In June of that year an article in the *New York Times* titled "Made in Japan Dilemma" was particularly prescient. The reporter captured the growing presence of Japan's industrialism in the form of imports into the U.S. markets with these remarks:

> Japan's pre-World War II ambition for major industrial status has become post-war policy. She has developed a number of highly specialized industries—among them cameras, sewing machines, and transistor radios for the consumer market, and scientific instruments, heavy equipment, and metals for industry.

Throughout that period of transformation the Japanese economy was surging and setting the table for a decade of stellar growth in the 1960s. As we shift our attention to the 1960s and what lies ahead for

Japan, let us take a look at the growth rates in GDP (gross domestic product), which measures the final market value of an economy's total goods and services. Generally speaking, GDP is a proxy for the growth of an economy and the health of its overall production. As can be seen in Figure 4.1, GDP increased in Japan at a staggering rate of 10.5 percent on average. Likewise, GDP in the United States provided far less to get excited about, as we can see in Figure 4.1 as we view the two sets of growth rates side by side.

As the figure illustrates, the Japanese economy was growing more than twice as fast the U.S. economy, yet this was largely unnoticed by the investing public. The transformation of Japan into an industrial power was tangible and detectable wholly aside from the simple anec-

Figure 4.1

Annual Growth in GDP of Japan and the United States, 1961–1970

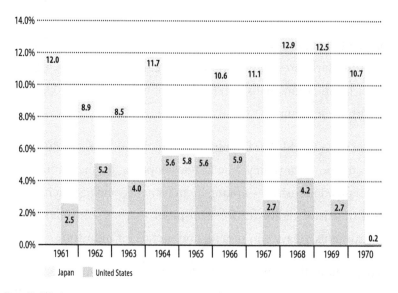

Source: World Bank

dotes related through press reports in the developed markets. For example, we will take a look at the transformation of Japan's export items in the period 1955–1968 in the figures and table below. As you examine Table 4.1, pay special attention to the declining percentage of textiles in Japan's exports and the rising percentage of machinery. You may notice that the growth rate in machinery was 26 percent per year, or about 3.5 times faster than the growth rate in textile exports. This is the sign of an economy making good on its ambition to become an industrial player and leaving its "cheap stuff" image behind.

While Japan was building itself into an industrial powerhouse, the majority of the world, in particular its stock investors, were asleep at the wheel—with the exception of perhaps one investor.

Uncle John's impression of Japan after his postwar visit left him believing that that country and its people would advance back to industrial relevance through their recipe of frugality and a deeply ingrained work ethic. And why not? That recipe of heavy saving and

Table 4.1

Japanese Exports Valued on the Basis of Customs Clearance

	1955	1960	1968
Foodstuffs	6.3%	6.3%	3.3%
Textiles	37.2%	30.1%	15.2%
Non-ferrous metals, mining products	4.8%	4.2%	2.5%
Chemicals	5.1%	4.5%	6.2%
Metals	19.2%	13.8%	18.1%
Mechinery	13.7%	25.4%	43.6%
Others	13.7%	15.7%	11.1%
	100.0%	100.0%	100.0%

Source: *Financial Analysts Journal.*

a tireless work ethic is part of Uncle John's own recipe for business success. Back in the early 1950s he already had found an English-speaking broker in Japan and was investing his personal savings in the Japanese stock market. However, during the 1950s Uncle John had not invested his clients' money in Japan because at that time the country had capital controls that required investors to leave their money in Japan. In other words, investors could put their money in by investing in stocks but could not withdraw it from the country afterward. Uncle John accepted this risk to his personal savings but did not expose his investors to the same risk.

The reason he was willing to take on the risk of not being able to withdraw his funds was that he was confident that the country would continue to open its markets and allow foreign investment to flow more freely. Uncle John recognized that Japan was willing to compromise on some policies so that it could continue to be a player in the game of worldwide trade. He believed that in time Japan would open its markets further and allow for the easier movement of foreign capital flows from investors outside the country. This included allowing foreign stock market investors to withdraw their money from the country. This was necessary for Japan to realize its strong ambition of becoming an industrial leader.

In the early 1960s, Uncle John's belief came to fruition as Japan rescinded some of its restrictions on foreign investors withdrawing their funds. When Japan finally pulled those restrictions on foreign investors in its stock market, Uncle John immediately jumped on the opportunity to begin investing his clients' funds in the Japanese market. Experienced and novice bargain hunters alike will appreciate why Uncle John jumped into Japanese equities headfirst when they consider that the stocks he found were trading at a P/E ratio of only 4× his estimate of earnings. Conversely, stocks in the United States were trading at a P/E of around 19.5× in that period. Let us pause for a moment and consider this comparison in more detail.

In the early 1960s, the Japanese economy was growing at an average rate of 10 percent and the U.S. economy was growing at an average rate of around 4 percent. In other words, the Japanese economy was expanding 2.5 times faster than the U.S. economy, but many stocks in Japan cost 80 percent less than the average of stocks in the United States (4× P/E versus 19.5× P/E). These are tremendous discrepancies, particularly when we consider investors' long-standing love affair with high-growth companies. How could such a discrepancy in the pricing of assets exist? There are many cited reasons. The reasons relate to the prevailing conventional wisdom at the time or simple misunderstandings. The first reason is that investing overseas, particularly somewhere as exotic as Japan in the 1960s, was basically too avant-garde for the time. In a report written for the *Financial Analysts Journal* in the late 1960s, the director of research for Daiwa Securities (a large Japanese brokerage), Shintaro Sakata, offered the reasons he heard most often for why foreign investors avoided Japan. Bargain hunters reading these citations will understand almost instantaneously why Uncle John found the Japanese market of the 1960s so attractive, in addition to its obviously superior growth rates and low P/E ratios.

"Fluctuations in stock prices are too extreme."

"There is not enough information."

Believe it or not, those are direct quotations. As we can see, two of the main objections among active investors who corresponded with Mr. Sakata were the exact things that Uncle John looked for in his search for bargains around the world. Ironically, these two character-istics that kept investors away from Japan were the very things Uncle John found attractive in an investment environment. Furthermore, these are just the reasons offered by professional investors. There was another, broader layer of negative sentiment among the public in the developed markets. That public sentiment was something along the lines of "Why would anyone invest in Japan? After all, they lost the war. They make trinkets in their low-wage factories and could never match the power and might of the United States in business." Those biases against the Japanese were inaccurate, unfair, and ignorant. Most important to the bargain hunter, though, without their existence the prices of those stocks would not have been so low relative to the intrin-sic worth of their companies. If everyone knew what Uncle John knew—that these were the cheapest stocks on earth based on his care-ful study—Japanese stocks would have ceased to be cheap as the crowd caught on and they became popular among investors.

With the benefit of hindsight, we can see how myopic and shel-tered the prevailing attitudes were toward Japan. The philosopher Kierkegaard once said, "We live life forward and understand it back-ward"; this is all too relevant to investing. These gaping misconcep-tions are the pitfalls of conventional wisdom. However, they usually have broad appeal in that they are supported by the majority. If you defy conventional wisdom, you probably will be chided for breaking from the pack. If you adopt conventional wisdom as your investment strategy, you will never achieve better results than the crowd.

Welcome to the world of neglected stocks. This realm is one of your most cherished sanctuaries as a bargain hunter. In many cases, when you are exploiting neglected stocks, you are not necessarily dealing with a large array of "problems" at the company level or even the industry level. Instead, you are tackling a heavy misconception or the mere obscurity of a stock in the broader market. You might question how the market could overlook or ignore what was occurring in Japan at the time and chalk it up to the "unsophisticated" nature of investors in the 1960s. You might believe that these situations no longer occur in the modern market. If you are headed down that intellectual path, you will get your chance to reconsider your argument when we discuss the South Korean market of the late 1990s and early 2000s in Chapter 8.

The point is that investors can create negative biases against stocks, industries, stock markets, and asset classes. Those biases serve as a set of blinders that keep investors from even considering bargain ideas. If you spot these stocks or, better yet, countries full of stocks and are tempted to move on and look at something more popular, stop yourself immediately. If you do not take the time to investigate the situation and size it up for yourself, you are passively investing along with the crowd. Sometimes the best opportunities are in plain view, but when investors see other investors passing them by or deriding them, they too pass. Social proof is a powerful force, but work hard not to let it guide your investment decisions. Often, what can happen—and what did happen in the case of Japan in the 1950s and 1960s—is that the entire economy can be transformed unnoticed by the crowd simply because they were unwilling to look in that direction.

That was what happened in Japan. The fundamental shifts that created the modern Japan were developing in the two decades after that nation's devastation from World War II, not in the 1970s and 1980s. By the time the results showed up in the 1970s and 1980s, the crowd was 10 steps behind Uncle John, who already had created a fortune for investors and was scouring the world for new opportunities.

Another way to think about this relationship between economic fundamentals is that they are similar to a tsunami, a tidal wave caused by a deep sea underground earthquake hundreds of miles from shore. In the case of Japan, the earthquake occurred in the 1950s when the country began to rebuild itself. In the two decades that followed, the tidal wave was traveling quietly beneath the ocean's surface. By the time the wider majority of the market caught on to what was happening and became excited about the country, the wave was about to hit shore and end in a crash. If you had waited until the broader stock market accepted Japan as an economic juggernaut in the 1980s, you were running with the crowd and heading straight to the edge of a cliff. In neglected stocks, these earthquakes happen all the time, but you have to be miles out from shore looking for them while the rest of the market inhabits a sunny and pleasant beach and waits for the next big thing.

You are going to need some psychological artillery for the battle you are undertaking as an investor in neglected stocks. The problem with neglected stocks is that they reward *patience*. The wait literally can be several years. In the case of Uncle John, his performance caught the full benefit of his 1960s prescience in the late 1960s and the 1970s as his performance surged ahead of that of U.S. fund managers. Purchasing neglected stocks is a lot like fishing: Sometimes you know where the fish are and know exactly what bait to use but still have to sit around and wait for a bite. They may not be biting because of current conditions, but conditions change. You cannot predict when the fish will bite. You cannot tell the fish when to bite, but when they finally do start to bite, you will clean up and be the envy of all fishers.

To give you a feel for the possible length of the wait and show you how long markets can take to catch on with outside observers, let us examine the growth in foreign investment in the Japanese stock market during the 1960s. Figure 4.2 shows two measures: the amount of U.S. dollars that was being invested in Japan and the percentage growth in the investment of those dollars. Because the Japanese stock market was still relatively underdeveloped and underutilized by its domestic investors as well as its corporations, those flows from the outside were able to affect the market. As you can see, in 1968 foreigners increased their investment over 370 percent in one year's time. This is a powerful illustration of why it pays to sit and wait after you have found a good bargain. The rush of money was so dramatic that those who were not invested could have caught it only toward the end and would have forfeited substantial gains while watching on the sidelines. Anecdotal evidence suggests that the wave of investment came from Europeans rather than Americans.

Figure 4.2

Foreign Gross Portfolio Investments in Japan, 1961–1970

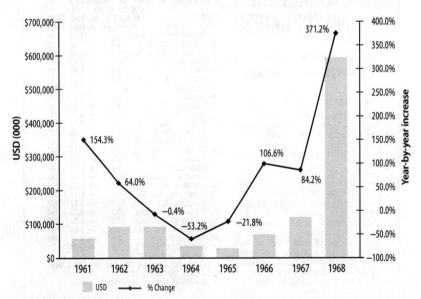

Source: *Financial Analysts Journal*

For Uncle John in particular, the wait and the patience it required paid off handsomely. As the stock market in the United States sank in the late 1960s, the Templeton Growth Fund was just starting to heat up. In some respects, the rise in Japanese equities over the ensuing decades signaled his arrival on the international stage of investing. Notice was served in January 1969 (see Figure 4.3).

To provide a broader and longer time frame for the benefits of spotting and investing in the Japanese stock market in the early 1960s, you can examine the TOPIX index of Tokyo stocks to get an idea of the market's performance once the economic reality became better known (see Figure 4.4).

Figure 4.3

The Templeton Growth Fund in 1969

TEMPLETON FUND 1969'S TOP GAINER

Up 19% in Lipper Study— Group Down on Average

By ROBERT D. HERSHEY Jr.

The Templeton Growth Fund, Inc., a small Toronto-based fund that is not currently offering shares to the public, ran away with top prize in the mutual fund performance sweepstakes for 1969, data compiled by the Arthur Lipper Mutual Fund Performance Analysis Service disclosed yesterday.

Templeton, with assets of only $6.7-million, registered a gain of 19.38 per cent in net asset value a share last year and surged from 19th position in 1968 to the top of a list of 376 funds surveyed by the Lipper organization.

The Top 25 Mutual Funds in 1969 (A)
Ranked in Order of Performance
Total net assets

1969 Rank.	Fund.	at 9/30/69 (in millions)	% chge. in 1969.	1968 Rank.
1.	Templeton Gr. Fd.$	6.7	+19.38	19
2.	Loomis-S. C. & I..	21.0	+11.04	89
3.	United F. C. & I..	10.0	+10.76	123
4.	Vantage-Ten-N. F..	0.9	+ 8.62	(B)
5.	Conn. W. Mutual..	0.5	+ 7.60	11
6.	Insur. & Bk. S. F.	2.9	+ 6.22	31
7.	Chemical Fund ..	532.0	+ 5.89	273
8.	Scudder I. Invest.	16.2	+ 5.54	98
9.	Trustees' Eq. Fund	2.7	+ 5.12	34
10.	Natl. Inv. Corp...	735.0	+ 4.38	253
11.	Natl. Western Fd..	0.3	+ 3.93	126
12.	T. Rowe P. G. Stk.	556.9	+ 3.68	251
13.	W. L. Morgan G. F.	14.2	+ 3.30	(B)
14.	Canadian Fund ..	27.8	+ 3.14	145
15.	Boston C. S. Fund.	35.7	+ 2:15	62
16.	Rochester Fund ..	0.4	+ 1.91	(B)
17.	David L. Babson I.	25.4	+ 1.34	118
18.	Johnston Mut. Fd.	129.9	+ 0.53	259
19.	Mass. Inv. Gr. Stk.	1201.1	+ 0.17	301
20.	Investors Sel. Fund	30.9	— 0.13	277
21.	Putnam Inv. Fund.	293.7	— 0.35	190
22.	Horace Mann Fund.	11.4	— 0.38	238
23.	Berkshire Gr. Fd..	1.0	— 0.65	(B)
24.	Pro Fund	18.7	— 0.69	255
25.	Decathlon Fund ..	1.8	— 0.77	(B)

Average size—$149.1.

(A)—Funds covered for the full 1968 year total 309; for 1969, 376.

(B)—Fund not in existence.

Figure 4.4

TOPIX Index of Stocks (Tokyo Exchange, December 1959–December 1989)

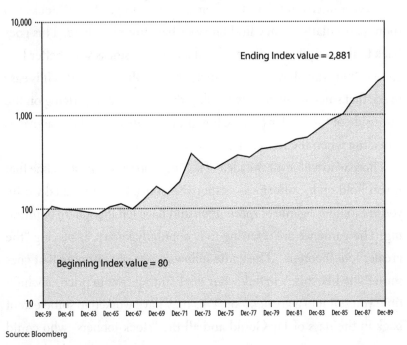

Source: Bloomberg

It is not hard to see the substantial appreciation in the market index over the 30 years after Uncle John first invested in Japan. In total the TOPIX Index of stocks on the Tokyo exchange increased 36 times from its December 31, 1959, value of 80 to its December 31, 1989, value of 2,881. Most investors and observers in the market like to dream of the occasional "10-bagger" that occurs when they purchase a stock and its value increases 10 times from the original value. In this case, we can see the sheer might of investing in neglected stocks as this index of stocks increased 36 times from its original value. Of course, Uncle John would be the first to tell you that he took the large majority of his investments out of Japan many years before it reached its peak at the end of the 1980s.

Some might take issue with the thought of "leaving money on the table" and exiting an investment too soon. Seasoned bargain hunters, however, understand that it is their common plight to sell stocks too soon, particularly as they find cheaper bargains elsewhere. This goes back to the simple discipline of replacing your stocks with better bargains as they rise above your estimate of what they are worth. It is easy to see that since we were able to take advantage of a mispricing on the downside of the stock when we bought it, it can and will rise above its fair value when the market falls in love with it.

Those who still resist the idea of selling "too soon" must realize that if you hold on to your stocks as they rise above their estimated worth, you are joining a game of *speculation* and have left the sphere of *investing*. The game we are referring to is popularly known as playing "the greater fool theorem." The game follows a line of reasoning that goes something like this: You hold your stock until it rises in price, at which time you sell it to a greater fool. This may have worked to some extent back in the days of Jay Gould and all the "stock jobbers" who could corner, overrun, or dump their stocks on unsuspecting marks, but the prospects for accomplishing it today are not good unless you like prison food. In any case, bargain hunters find the idea of the greater fool theorem foolish from top to bottom. The whole strategy is underpinned by arrogance and some unexplained notion of market timing. Furthermore, arrogance in the market will get you killed 10 times out of 10. You may escape for a while, perhaps even years, but eventually your hubris will catch up with you and deal with you swiftly.

In the last few paragraphs we focused on the returns available from the market when we spot a large geographically dominated instance of neglected stocks, or what stock market people refer to as a country discount. However, as we mentioned in previous chapters, we are not interested in the "market" per se, because we are bargain hunters of stocks who construct larger baskets that come to represent a proxy of undervalued "markets" on a case-by-case, stock-by-stock basis. Now that we are shifting our focus to the company level, we can discuss another important tool in the arsenal of the bargain hunter. Up to this point we have focused on some of the larger misconceptions that determined equity prices in Japan in the 1960s. That is, we have discussed some of the biases and negative sentiments among foreigners that prevented investors from buying the stocks of Japanese firms.

However, there was another layer of misinformation about Japanese firms, and it had nothing to do with investors' attitudes. This was a blanket cast across the majority of the market that few investors understood at the time; it took years for investors to comprehend and exploit it. This layer of misinformation was created by the accounting regulations that guided the way Japanese firms reported their income. The last sentence may have spooked some of you, but rest assured that we are not going to launch into an academic treatise on international accounting standards. Instead, we think you will agree that the layer of misinformation was created by a simple and rudimentary discrepancy that savvy bargain hunters could spot.

Let us take the best example of a widely known company that Uncle John invested in where he took advantage of this accounting inefficiency. Most readers have heard of the large, well-known Japanese electronics company Hitachi. Hitachi was actually a collection of companies. In other words, most people see Hitachi as a singular entity, but in fact it represents a group of companies owned by the parent company, which is called Hitachi. Think of Hitachi as an umbrella with many separate subsidiary companies lying beneath it that Hitachi owns outright.

As a result of the accounting regulations at that time, the earnings being generated by the companies that Hitachi owned were not reported on Hitachi's financial statements. Therefore, the price of Hitachi's stock divided by the parent company's earnings (which did not reflect the earnings of the companies it owned) created a P/E ratio that was falsely high. Uncle John understood that when he bought Hitachi, he was buying the entire collection of companies that it owned, not just the parent company. Therefore, when he made his estimation of the value of the entire company, including all the smaller companies it owned, and compared it with the market price, there was a tremendous difference between what he saw and what the average investor who did not make that calculation saw. Put another way, Hitachi *supposedly* traded at a price/earnings ratio of 16 (share price divided by earnings per share = 16). However, if you divided the share price by the earnings per share reported by the company *and* all the companies Hitachi owned, the stated share price divided by the new amount of earnings plummeted to 6× from 16×.

What Uncle John was doing in his analysis was consolidating the earnings of the parent, which were nominal, with the earnings of all the companies owned by the parent, which were substantial. After all, by purchasing a share of Hitachi, he was taking fractional ownership of Hitachi and everything that came with it, including those subsidiary companies. The "everything that came with it" was far more valuable than the parent company called Hitachi. Eventually the Japanese regulators changed the accounting rules and made parent companies report their consolidated earnings in addition to their parent earnings. That change shone a light on the hidden value among the various listed parent companies, and investors began to bid their prices higher in response.

What we have illustrated here is a major blow to the argument for not investing in Japan because there is not enough information. In this case, it was true that there was not enough information; however, that played to Uncle John's advantage because he took the time and made the effort to understand the situation from top to bottom. The key point here is not to invest blindly in situations in which information is lacking; instead, we want to illustrate the benefits of not dismissing a potential bargain out of hand and the importance of the doctrine of the extra ounce. In this case the payoffs were substantial. Similarly, there is a payoff to *not* investing in situations that look like bargains when in fact they are not. In other words, there is a nasty flip side to not doing your homework when you invest in a stock.

Often these situations arise from accounting treatments not unlike the virtuous one that existed in Japan. However, they also can take on a menacing form when the items that are not detected are liabilities rather than assets. Look no further than the present-day American poster child of opaque accounting, Enron. In the case of Enron, it was also a matter of "businesses" not reported in the financial statements, but in this case the businesses were shells that were funneling money to the executives and hiding the scary truth from investors. In the Enron case, the company was worthless instead of being worth more. In either case, bargain hunters should not run from misinformation but embrace it and seek the truth. Ignoring details can lead to mistakes in either situation: passing over Japan or investing in Enron.

This discussion of Japanese accounting practices illuminates a microcosmic inefficiency that worked in conjunction with the larger macrocosmic inefficiency involving investor attitudes. The point is that there is no substitute for challenging the belief system that is determining the price of an asset. Some readers may feel a bit overwhelmed by this discussion of accounting and the other surprises that await them in future investments, but the world is full of accounting-oriented people who eat this stuff up. If the word *accounting* makes your head hurt or scares you, outsource the job to someone who loves it. The mutual funds you invest in should have plenty of analysts on staff who can see through opaque accounting and detect hidden opportunities. Please note, though, that it will pay you to make sure that the investment professionals you hire are protecting your assets with these perspectives. Before you hire someone to choose stocks for you, ask that person how he or she goes about these tasks and what he or she safeguards against.

With this discussion on the inefficiencies created by the foreign investors' view of Japan as well as the opaque accounting methods out of the way, let us turn to what really attracted Uncle John to these stocks. The long and short of what Uncle John saw in the stocks was their low prices compared with their strong earning power and truly remarkable growth prospects. Put another way, he believed that the prices he paid for the stocks in Japan during the early 1960s in no way, shape, or form reflected the amount they would be worth over the many years to come. Basically, he spotted remarkably successful companies such as Toyota before anyone else knew that Japan's stock market was a legitimate place to invest. The companies he saw were very profitable and were growing their sales and earnings very quickly, especially in comparison to a benchmark such as the United States.

Before we get into the mechanics and methods of Uncle John's purchases in Japan, let us address some popular nomenclature that can be confusing. First and foremost, almost everyone has heard or developed some notion that there are different types of investors who have different styles. The most popularly cited of these distinctions is that stock investors fall into one of two camps: value investing or growth investing. As popular convention would have it, a *value investor* is someone who typically is thought to invest in slower-growing, mature industries. Conversely, a *growth investor* is someone who invests in newer companies and is far less concerned with the price he or she pays for stocks because he or she is tapping into companies that are about to set the world on fire. If you have these preconceived notions or use these classifications and are looking to place Uncle John in one of these categories, you need to adjust your perspective.

Uncle John's main goal is to buy something for substantially less than its worth. If that means purchasing something with limited growth potential, that is okay; if it means buying something that should grow at a double-digit clip for the next 10 years, that is even better. If the company is growing, the point is to avoid paying for the growth. Growth in a company is a wonderful thing; your returns on a stock can go on for years if you spot good bargains in growing companies. However, this is not an excuse to pay too much. If you hypothesize that a company is about to knock the cover off the ball and be a long-term grower and then discover that the stock price has been bid up in anticipation of that growth, move on. There is no reward for getting the fundamentals right if they already are built into the stock price. As a bargain hunter, you should be focused on extreme mismatches between the way a stock is priced and what it is worth, not simple nuances. These mismatches can occur in any type of company, at least from time to time. Thus, as a successful bargain hunter you must remain an agnostic about the superficial distinction between a value investor and a growth investor and resist creating biases that prevent you from spotting bargains.

Now let us return to the specific stocks in Japan and how Uncle John reasoned that they represented good bargains at the time. One example of a stock that Uncle John bought in Japan was Ito-Yokado, a large supermarket chain. This stock had a price/earnings ratio of 10 and was growing its earnings at 30 percent a year while Japan was developing into a mature industrial nation. He reasoned that this looked like a good bargain because the price he was paying for future earnings was probably far less than what he would pay elsewhere for the same thing. The process that helped lead to that conclusion included a tool familiar to most bargain hunters: *comparison shopping*. Uncle John reasoned that by purchasing Ito-Yokado, he was getting a far better deal than what was available in other markets when he compared Ito-Yokado with the large, well-known developed market supermarket Safeway. To arrive at that conclusion, he compared the prices he would pay for a dollar of future probable earnings with the estimated long-term growth rates in those earnings. Making this judgment requires the simple application of a ratio popularly known as the PEG (price/earnings to growth) ratio. The PEG ratio is simply the price/earnings ratio of the stock divided by the long-term estimate of growth in earnings. In this case we can take the respective P/E ratios of Ito-Yokado and Safeway, divide them by their reasonably expected future growth rates in earnings, and roughly compare what we are paying for the companies' future growth prospects. We illustrate this exercise below:

Ito-Yokado
Price/earnings = 10×
Estimated growth = 30%
PEG = P/E (10) ÷ estimated growth (30) = 0.3

Safeway
Price/earnings = 8×
Estimated growth = 15%
PEG = P/E (8) ÷ estimated growth = 0.5

Because the PEG ratio we calculate for Ito-Yokado is less than the PEG ratio we calculate for Safeway, we should consider Ito-Yokado a better bargain in spite of the relationship we see between the two companies' respective P/E ratios. The notion here is that we actually are paying less for Ito-Yokado because the growth rate in its future probable earnings is much higher.

However, it is very important that as a bargain hunter you pay close attention to the reasonableness of these growth assumptions. You must maintain your skeptical edge in processing information when you consider these relationships. For instance, a stock with a P/E of 30 and an estimated growth rate of 100 percent in its future earnings per share also has a PEG of 0.3. You must ask yourself candidly, Is this a reasonable assumption? Is it probable that earnings will grow that fast? It is not, or at least the odds are heavily stacked against that. It pays to question the relationships and assumptions that constitute these ratios actively. Ratios are not necessarily the beginning and end to investing unless you have investigated everything in between and trust that the relationship is true. In other words, it is incumbent on you to investigate whether you really are paying the least amount of money possible for the most likely future prospects for the company.

Always take a ratio and interpret what it implies. Break it down into its components and scrutinize them. Perhaps the P/E itself is flawed in the PEG. For instance, a P/E of 10× for a company whose estimate of earnings per share (the E in P/E) is expected to grow 5 percent may be more reasonable than a P/E of 10× when the earnings per share needs to increase 50 percent to make a ratio of 10×. Blindly purchasing stocks with low PEGs is no more effective than blindly purchasing all the stocks you can find with low P/Es because it exposes you to avoidable mistakes. In the case of Ito-Yokado, the estimated growth rate of 30 percent may seem a bit optimistic, but at the same time this was a company standing on the verge of many decades of expansion. Uncle John was investing in the notion that the Japanese would continue to raise their per capita incomes (the amount of income each citizen earns) and consequently adapt consumption patterns that were more analogous to those of consumers in developed markets such as the United States and Europe.

More important than the fundamental interpretation of Ito-Yokado's prospects is the realization that comparison shopping for bargains is an important tool in the bargain hunter's repertoire. Uncle John always said that there are 100 yardsticks of value that an analyst can use to judge the worth of a stock, but this is one of the techniques that he employed over and over. Also, this technique lends itself well to the strategy of always staying invested in the best bargains available. By making these relative value-based judgments, you are constantly assessing the attractiveness of your investments in relation to what is available in the market.

This practice of comparison is a highly useful tool in approaching what is probably the most difficult question in investing: when to sell a stock. Uncle John spent many years considering this question, and the answer he came up with and applied to his professional and personal investments was "when you have found a much better stock to replace it." This practice of comparison is a productive exercise because it makes the decision to sell far easier than it is when you focus on the stock and the company in isolation. When a stock price is approaching your assessment of what it is worth, that is a good time to be searching for a possible replacement. During your normal routine of searching, you may find a stock whose price is far lower than your appraisal of the business, at which time you may elect to replace your holding. However, this practice should be accompanied by some discipline and is not an excuse to become whimsical or turn over your portfolio unnecessarily.

To prevent the possibility of churning your stocks and creating wasteful activity, Uncle John recommends that you purchase a replacement only when you have found a stock that is 50 percent better. In other words, if you are holding a stock that has been successful as a holding and it is trading at $100 and you think it is worth only $100, you may be inclined to purchase a new stock that is undervalued by 50 percent. For instance, you may have located new shares that trade at $25, but you think they are worth $37.50; in that case you should replace your prior holding at $100 (which you believe is worth 0 percent more than the price) with the new shares that you have located at $25 (which you believe are worth 50 percent more than the price).

Employing this discipline successfully—that is, continuously searching for better bargains than what you currently hold—will give you the process and the psychological equipment needed to avoid getting swept up in the euphoria that is driving the prices of the shares you hold higher. The thrill of locating more bargains should be far more rewarding than sitting back and relishing your recent successes. This idea is embedded in the notion that focusing on the future is more important than focusing on the past.

Professional bargain hunters are a lot like professional athletes: Everyone is judging you on the last trade you made or the last shot you took. To have staying power in the game, you must remain focused on the next opportunity. That said, this process of searching for relative bargains guided Uncle John out of Japan before it ended in a disastrous crash. By the time Japan had caught on in full force with the investing public and become extensively popular, Uncle John had reduced his holdings in Japan from 60 percent of his portfolio to less than 2 percent. As we can see, this mechanical, quantitative process of comparing bargains with one another should continuously push you into the best bargains available and out of harm's way. You will have the necessary perspective to sidestep or ignore the hype and remain a step ahead of the crowd, which is the constant modus operandi of the bargain hunter.

For Uncle John the decision to exit Japan was simple; he was finding better bargains in Canada, Australia, and the United States. There was no qualitative factor that guided the decision; instead, the decision was predicated on the simple calculations of stock prices compared with the values of the companies. Applying qualitative reasoning in this decision-making process would have muddled his judgment, and maintaining clear judgment is a central tenet in successful bargain hunting.

To get a better feel for how Uncle John executed this strategy and what the true variables were that propelled his decision-making process for exiting Japan, look at Figure 4.5, which illustrates the prices that the market paid for Japanese company earnings, which progressed higher over time. In viewing Figure 4.5, conceptualize the rising P/E ratios as being directly related to the amount of attention and hype that Japan increasingly garnered as its economic progress and strength became widely known. In other words, Japanese stocks were becoming the story stocks that bargain hunters consider toxic.

This view of the prices investors became willing to pay for earnings over time is illuminating for many reasons. First, it gives investors a glimpse into the progression of a market that began as hardly known or understood by anyone to one that became all the rage by the end of the 1980s, right before its collapse. This was the equivalent of going

Figure 4.5

TOPIX Index Price-to-Earnings Ratios

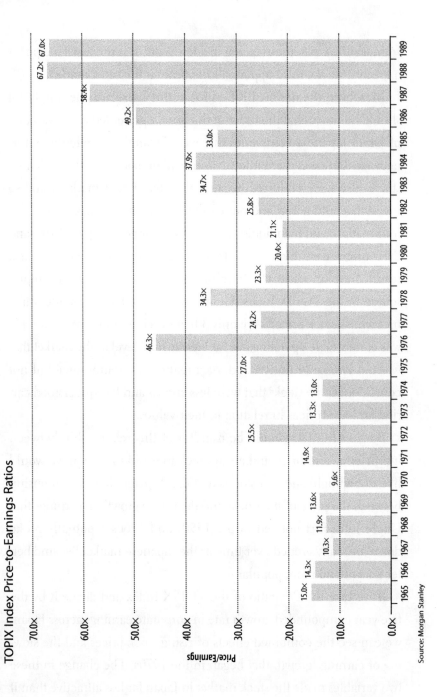

Source: Morgan Stanley

from wallflower to prom queen in a few years. It is not just a recipe for a Disney movie; this happens all the time in the stock market.

Moreover, the nominal P/E ratios in the figure are relevant, but it should be noted that the index at the time represented a narrow band of larger Japanese companies that were favored by foreign investors because there was more information available on those stocks. Those stocks also were preferred because they had larger markets, and so investors could get in and out easily. This visibility, large amount of information, and high liquidity increased their general popularity, and their prices were higher in relation to their earnings per share as a result. In many cases Uncle John was purchasing stocks not represented in the TOPIX Index. He was finding better values in companies whose stock prices were only 3 to 4x their earnings per share. He was comfortable operating at a "subterranean" level of the market that was not known or understood. As a matter of circumstance but not coincidence, the stocks that were less known and less understood carried far lower prices in relation to their values.

Bargain hunters should be mindful of this relationship between inefficiency and price and always seek to exploit it. What we would like to highlight and focus on is that the disparate initial relationship between the price of the stocks and the future growth in earnings that Uncle John first noticed in the 1950s and 1960s eventually broke down and fully eroded over time as the Japanese market became better known and more popular.

If we take the P/E ratio of the TOPIX Index and divide it by the five-year compounded growth rate in corporate earnings across Japan, we can see the combined effects of rising stock prices and the slowing of earnings growth that began in the 1970s. The change in these two variables made the stock market in Japan far less attractive than it was when Uncle John first began to invest in it. It also produced more attractive *relative bargains* in other markets around the world. Figure 4.6 provides an arithmetical representation of the basic phenomena that led Uncle John out of Japan and into other more attractive bargain markets elsewhere over the course of the 1970s. Two basic developments led to the increase in the PEG ratio for Japanese stocks over the decade: The stock prices and P/E ratios rose as Japan gained in popularity, and the phenomenal growth rate in earnings that attracted Uncle John to the stocks began to slow dramatically. In effect, the investors who continued to pile into the market were paying more and more but getting less and less as the decade wore on.

Figure 4.6

TOPIX Index Representative PEG Ratio

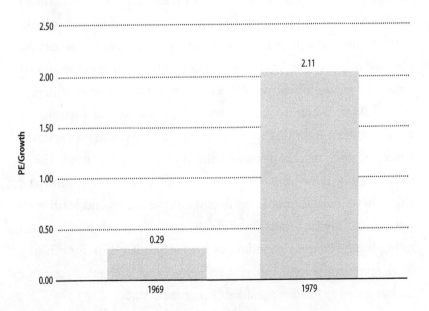

Sources: Morgan Stanley, Ministry of Internal Affairs and Communications

Eventually, the broader public became increasingly aware of Japan and the economic transformation that had occurred over the previous few decades. The result of that belated awareness was that by the 1980s an era of hyper enthusiasm developed in the market for Japanese shares. The prices that investors paid for assets such as stocks and real estate progressively increased and reached levels that could not be considered probable but were instead fantastical. The reasons behind this strong upward trajectory in asset prices during the late 1980s were numerous. First, many untrained investors developed a purchasing strategy that was based on a myth that the stock market would only go up, and as in any market bubble, there were a number of local brokers and salespeople deemphasizing any notion of risk or loss. Often, the cause of higher prices in the market was the simple fact that prices had gone higher the day before. The large majority of the buyers who drove prices higher were incentivized to continue buying by the assumed wealth they were creating in their brokerage accounts on a daily basis.

What made this phenomenon particularly dangerous was that the assumed paper wealth being created stimulated consumerism among those who thought their wealth could support a new level of luxurious behavior. When the market crashed on the back of interest rate increases, those individuals were taught a difficult lesson on the flimsy nature of stock market prices. By the time all this occurred, Uncle John was long gone from the Japanese market, but he obviously paid close attention to it in order to document the events and learn from the public folly that unfolded. Observing these events and incorporating these vicarious experiences helped prepare him for a future stock market bubble that we discuss in the coming chapters, one that he harnessed to make a remarkably profitable trade.

Chapter | 5

THE DEATH OF EQUITIES OR THE BIRTH OF A BULL MARKET?

The death of equities looks like an almost permanent condition.
–*Business Week*, August 1979

"The death of equities" sounds a bit dramatic, to say the least. If someone looked you in the eye and told you that stocks were becoming obsolete or would permanently fall out of favor, how would you react? Does that statement seem ridiculous? If so, welcome to the world of hindsight, where our ability to recognize folly is unfettered and our vision is 20/20. When that comment was made, could you have seen it as overblown? The reason we ask is that this opinion had real teeth among the investing public as the 1970s came to a close. It was backed by the good evidence of a miserable decade in the U.S. stock market. The market literally moved sideways for a decade throughout the 1970s, and there were some nasty corrections along the way. In other words, you could have been invested in the market for 10 years with very little to show for it when 1980 finally arrived. If you dared to compare your returns with the rate of inflation in the United States, you probably would have felt utterly defeated.

In contrast, if you had invested in commodities, real estate, or collectibles, you probably would have felt a bit smarter, since those investments effectively store value against inflation and preserve purchasing power. You could have pointed to your much better returns in those "tangible" investments or regretted not having gotten into them sooner and joined the chorus of investors singing about a new age in investing. The new age was predicated on the successful returns that were being generated in commodity-related investments. In typical fashion, a set of investors took recent historical events and projected them forward, except that in this case they took the extreme view that those investments would be in vogue forever. The age of new investing was proclaimed with bold conviction. There it was on the cover of an issue of *Business Week* in August 1979: "The Death of Equities."

Of course, nearly 30 years later the magazine cover and the article penned on this theme are thought of mostly as a joke. Many point to the cover as a fantastic buy signal for the stock market and an equally good time to exit commodities. Bargain hunters in the stock market should have taken the magazine cover and the views that supported it as a point of maximum pessimism The market in 1979 and the three years that followed represented a state of nirvana for bargain hunters. To see just how pessimistic investors had become, let's dig into the article and flesh out some of the ideas that were embraced at that time. The article opened as follows:

> The masses long ago switched from stocks to investments having higher yields and more protection from inflation. Now the pension

funds—the market's last hope—have won permission to quit stocks and bonds for real estate, futures, gold, and even diamonds. The death of equities looks like an almost permanent condition—reversible someday, but not soon.

This introduction to the article is a great study in the elements to look for when you want to buy at the bottom. Wise bargain hunters should view the article's message as a bullish indicator, rather than a bearish one. The first clue comes in the opening sentence: "The masses long ago switched from stocks to investments having higher yields." First and foremost, bargain hunters are not looking to follow the masses anywhere, period. Instead, bargain hunters go exactly where the masses are not because that is the best place to spot a bargain. The next great clue lies in the words "the death of equities looks like an almost permanent condition." Uncle John was asked about finding the point of maximum pessimism, and his advice was "to wait until the ninety-ninth person out of a hundred gives up."

From that point the only buyer left is you, and the market for the stock can only go up because there are no sellers left. This is difficult to gauge, but when the consensus is that "the death of equities looks like an almost permanent condition," it is easy to sense the level of despair and pessimism surrounding the market. Moreover, there was pretty good evidence in this excerpt that the market was approaching a point of maximum pessimism: "Now the pension funds—the market's last hope—have won permission to quit stocks and bonds for real estate, futures, gold, and even diamonds."

When we think about this statement, it appears to be saying that the last holdouts in stocks are ready to sell. So if we have reached a point where the last group of sellers is exiting the market, can prices fall much more after they finish selling? No. If the last batch of sellers leaves the market, you must have a keen eye to be the buyer on the other side. Once all the sellers are gone, logically, there are only buyers left in the market. Conversely, what about commodities? They had been on a good run, and now the last group of buyers was coming into that market. Once they were in, who else was left to buy commodities and bid them higher? No one. It should not be taken as a coincidence that the commodities market and the stock market were on the verge of trading places once the last group of sellers in one became the last group of buyers in the other. This is an example of the mechanical logic that underlies contrarian investing.

If these statements made you think that the stock market was teeming with bargains, you are exactly right and are thinking like a bargain hunter. Before we get to that, however, there is some important ground to cover. If you study market manias over time, there is a certain ideology that inevitably rears its ridiculous head in every instance. We are not sure what causes these people to be so outspoken in their views, but they appear like clockwork whenever the market gets carried away in one direction or the other. More often you see this stuff when the market is extremely overpriced or in a bubble. It has long been known, however, that the stock market's pessimism drives prices down at least as much as it drives them up during a fit of euphoria.

In this sense, it is not surprising to find a certain statement emerging during "the death of equities" stock market bottom. The statement we are referencing contains the misguided notion that the financial paradigm has changed and the market has entered a *new period* in which stock prices and company values are no longer relevant: "We have entered a new financial age. The old rules no longer apply."

If and when you read these statements in the future, they should activate every alarm, bell, and whistle in your bargain-hunting soul. These words and the myopic concepts that back them are the antithesis of wise bargain hunting. Statements like these crop up from time to time in cases of extreme moves in market prices over a prolonged period. Usually they appear as an attempt to justify paying too much for an asset. In this case the pundits were defending a "new age" of investing in real estate and commodities. If this statement does not strike a chord, perhaps we need to supplement it. The companion statement that always seems to accompany this reasoning is "Only the elderly who have not understood the changes in the nation's financial markets, or who are unable to adjust to them, are sticking with stocks."

Where to begin? This statement is wrong on so many different levels. However, as we will see when we discuss the U.S. technology bubble of the late 1990s, the new age investors often take jabs at the older investors "who are being left behind." As bargain hunters, we know better than to second-guess our elders who have seen it all and done it all in the market. Being an older investor is rarely a hindrance and often an advantage. Knowledge and experience as a bargain hunter scale with age; the longer you are in the game, the better you get. Finally, it is ironic that "the elderly who have not understood the changes in the nation's financial markets" were the only ones smart enough to be long in stocks at the bottom of the market. They were not behind the game; they were actually ahead of it.

For some reason this collection of statements seems to be directed toward value investors and comes accompanied by a snicker. Perhaps as bargain hunters we take special issue with these jabs, but whatever the reason, we will save the rest of that discussion for the sixth chapter on the technology bubble of the late 1990s. Regardless of the period or the market involved, history has always shown that statements like these are the pinnacle of folly. The simple fact is that the relationship between asset prices and asset values always applies, and you ignore that relationship at your own peril.

If there was ever an instance of maximum pessimism that was broadcast clearly for all to see, it was the U.S. stock market as it closed the 1970s and began the 1980s. By the time 1980 rolled around, Uncle John had 60 percent of his funds invested in the United States. That was in stark contrast to the stock market consensus of the time, which was that equities were dying on the vine thanks to runaway inflation. Investors ran away from U.S. stocks as if they were a building on fire, but Uncle John took the opposite approach and calmly walked in the front door to size up the damage. He did benefit from a fresh perspective on the market since he had not been riding U.S. stocks down into the pit of despair along with everyone else over the previous 10 years. Quite the opposite; he had just finished piggybacking the Japanese market's gains to become the most successful mutual fund manager of the decade.

Why was Uncle John so bullish on American stocks when no one else would touch them with a 10-foot pole? One part of the answer is simple: No one would touch them with a 10-foot pole. The second part is that this prevailing attitude left some of the best-known, most-heralded companies in the United States, members of the Dow, trading at historical lows relative to earnings as well as book value, among other measures.

In fact, Uncle John researched the matter and could not find an instance in the *history* of the U.S. market in which stocks had been cheaper. Keep in mind that this includes the Great Depression and the crash that began in 1929. To bear this out, we begin with a reference to a compilation of P/E (price/earnings) ratios put together by the research provider Value Line. In Table 5.1, we can judge by the P/E ratios calculated for the Dow Jones Industrial Average that the 1979 average P/E ratio of 6.8 was in fact the lowest mark on record. In contrast, Value Line's research shows that the long-term average P/E ratio for the Dow is 14.2×. In other words, the average P/E in the Dow over the course of 1979 was 52 percent lower than the long-term average going back to the 1920s.

Table 5.1

Top 10 Lowest Annual P/E Ratios for the Dow Jones Industrial Average

Rank	Year	P/E Ratio
1	1979	6.8
2	1950	7.0
3	1978	7.3
4	1980	7.3
5	1949	7.6
6	1974	7.7
7	1948	7.8
8	1981	8.2
9	1988	9.0
10	1924	9.2

Source: Value Line.

Almost as impressive as the 1979 P/E ratio of 6.8× on the Dow is the overall number of low-ratio years flanking 1979 in both the late 1970s and the early 1980s. This provides a good illustration of how negative the market had become and how that sentiment lasted over the course of several years. Investors had been put through the wringer by inflation, high interest rates, oil crises, a hostage crisis, and the new threat of Japanese competition. Investors were being beaten down from all directions, and both economic and psychological effects were showing up in stock prices.

The historically low P/E ratio of the Dow Jones was a traditional buy signal for bargain hunters in that period. However, there were buy signals coming from many different directions, and each of them led to the same conclusion: U.S. stocks were dirt cheap. Uncle John always stresses the importance of maintaining many different perspectives of value rather than just one, such as the P/E ratio. The death of equities market provides a good opportunity to highlight some of the techniques that Uncle John employed and that in the future could be adopted by bargain hunters.

Uncle John's approach to bargain hunting always involved being able to apply one of the "100 yardsticks of value" that were available to a securities analyst. There are two good reasons for taking this approach. The first and perhaps more important is that if you are limited to a single method of evaluating stocks, you periodically will go through times, even years, when your method does not work. This concept is analogous to why you should never invest solely in just one country's stock market for the lifetime of your investments. If you stick with one region, country, market, or industry, there will be periods when you will you underperform the market averages. Because of the limited selection of bargains that can be located with one measure such as the P/E ratio, you will feast or starve on the basis of that ratio alone. Thus, if you rely on only a P/E ratio to evaluate stocks, there will be times when you cannot find value with that measure, but perhaps you could have with another, such as the ratio of price to cash flow. For that matter, one cannot guarantee that your method for bargain hunting will not become obsolete.

Uncle John believes that all the stock selection methods that have proved to be successful over time become universally adopted and eventually cease to work when everyone practices them in unison. For instance, if you decided to adopt some of the widely proven methods of selection detailed in Benjamin Graham's *Security Analysis*, such as purchasing the stocks of companies whose market values are lower than their net working capital or inventory, you probably would have a hard time finding stocks that matched that description. At the very least you would have a much harder time than Graham did when he established the method and it was advertised as successful. In sum, if you have only one method for selecting bargains, you may miss obvious opportunities elsewhere.

The second good reason to use many yardsticks of value is to accumulate confirmation of your findings from different methods. If you can see that a stock is a bargain on five different measures, that should increase your conviction that the stock is a bargain. Raising your conviction level is an important psychological asset as you face the volatility of the stock market. With that said, we will take this opportunity to run through a few examples of other value measures and indicators that were cropping up during the late 1970s and early 1980s as equities were "dying."

These methods may be new to some readers and second nature to others, but at the very least they provide some perspective on the spirit of the bargain-hunting process and the many points of view that can be incorporated.

One of the many attractive qualities Uncle John found in the U.S. stock market of the late 1970s and early 1980s was that stock prices or market values had become thoroughly depressed relative to the asset values listed in the financial statements of different companies. The most widely known and practiced method of comparing a market value to an accounting asset value is the price/book ratio. In the simplest terms, this is the stock price of the company divided by the result of the total assets minus the total liabilities (the book value), which then is divided by the number of shares outstanding (to find assets minus liabilities per share and compare it to the share price). What bargain hunters look for when they calculate this ratio is a number that is low, perhaps around one or even below one.

The interpretation of the ratio is based on a view of what you are paying in the stock price for the amount listed as the net worth of the company in its financial statements. If you are paying a stock price that is lower than the amount listed as the worth of the company, you may be getting a bargain. Of course, the company may be running itself into the ground and the market has picked up on it; in that case, the stock price justifiably is below the book value or net worth per share. It is important to understand that when the ratio is one or below one, the stock market has *low expectations* for the business and that is being reflected in the stock price. Conversely, if the market believes that the company can generate a return on its equity that compensates it for the risk of investing in the stock, it will reward the stock with a price-to-book ratio above one and sometimes well above one, depending on how much it likes the stock. Here is a summary of the ratio:

Stock price ÷ book value per share = price/book ratio

Book value per share = (total assets − total liabilities) ÷ shares outstanding

This ratio has been around forever, but in the late 1970s and early 1980s a peculiar phenomenon was occurring in the U.S. economy: runaway double-digit inflation that eclipsed investing. The presence of double-digit inflation altered the conventional nature of the price/book ratio and uncovered extra value for investors.

For instance, because of double-digit inflation, Uncle John reasoned that although prices relative to book values were already enticingly low and therefore attractive to a bargain hunter, the ratio was not revealing the full picture of how discounted the stocks had become. He reasoned that the *replacement value* of assets was much higher than the historical costs of the assets listed on a company's balance sheet. In other words, if we ran a company with a plant that cost us $10 million to construct five years ago and the growth rate in prices—that is, inflation—has been increasing 15 percent a year since then, it would cost us far more than the $10 million we originally paid to replace the plant if we built it today. In fact, it probably would cost us around $20 million to reconstruct that plant as a result of the 15 percent growth in prices. One way to envision this is to think of what the plant is constructed of; let's say it's primarily steel. If the price of steel increases 15 percent a year from the year we built the plant, it would cost us a great deal more to replace the plant later because of the price increases.

Using this logic, we can see that stock prices not only were low relative to the historical costs of assets but were much lower than the costs of actually replacing those assets. Uncle John said that in late 1982, stock prices relative to the replacement values of assets *were at all-time historical lows*.

Figure 5.1 shows the price/book ratios of the Dow Jones Industrial Average companies going back to the 1920s, and we can see the historical importance of that ratio falling below one for several years beginning in 1978 and lasting through 1982. Moreover, when we consider that the rate of inflation over that period was in the teens, we can grasp how out of whack the prices of stocks were with their replacement values, since they were trading below even their historical costs. To bring this relationship into better focus, if we look across the graph and search for another period in which the Dow Jones price/book ratio was below one, we must go all the way back to 1932. That year was the low point of the market crash that began in 1929, and the country was in the middle of the Great Depression. However, during the Depression the economy experienced falling prices, known as *deflation*, versus the rising prices of the late 1970s and early 1980s, known as *inflation*. Thus, although in 1932 the Dow Jones had collapsed to one-ninth of its in September 1929 value, the index was not nearly the bargain it became during the "death of equities" period.

The reason the index of Dow stocks was not as good a bargain at the bottom of the Depression crash was that the replacement value of the assets held by Dow companies was 20 percent *below* the stated book value. In other words, if the respective owners of the Dow companies wanted to replace the assets owned by their companies, it would have cost them 20 percent *less* to do so because of falling prices. In the plainest terms, the values ascribed to a company's assets in 1932 were *overstated* on the basis of replacement value.

We could take the price/book ratio for the Dow in 1932, which was 0.79, and make a case that the true price/book ratio, using the replacement value of the assets, was closer to 1.0 when we wrote the value of the assets down to their replacement value. Conversely, if we reinterpreted the price/book ratios of the late 1970s and early 1980s in terms of their replacement costs, we would find that the costs to replace the assets were 70 percent above the stated book values of the assets. This was due to the rampant inflation that drove up the prices of nearly

Figure 5.1

Price-to-Book Annual Averages for the Dow Jones Industrial Average

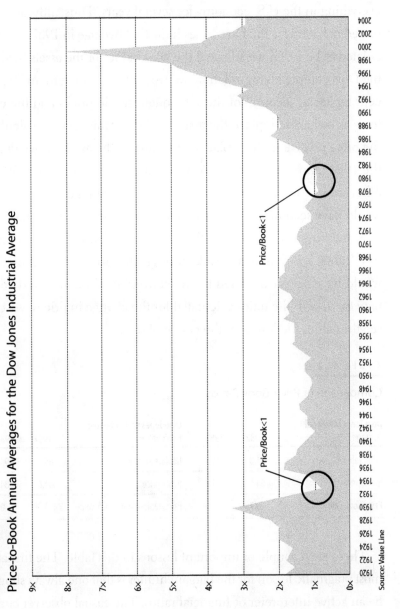

Source: Value Line

everything in the U.S. economy for several years. Thus, although the price/book ratio for the Dow Jones Industrial Average in 1982 was calculated to be 1.0, if we adjusted the book values of the assets held by the Dow companies for inflation, we would have valued them 70 percent higher to account for the subsequent rise in prices and the cost to us as owners to replace the assets. If we use this logic to calculate the price relative to the replacement value of the assets, as we did in the 1932 ratio, we find that the 1982 ratio falls from 1.0 to 0.59. In other words, stocks were 40 percent cheaper than a casual observer would have seen by examining only the standard price/book ratio.

Sometimes it is helpful to illustrate these relationships in a table (see Table 5.2).When we walk through the price/book ratios that would have been calculated by the conventional method and compare them with the ratios calculated for the change in prices, we can see the values hidden from the casual observer.

Table 5.2

Comparison of Price/Book Ratios

Dow Jones Industrial Average	1932	1982	Dow Jones with Adjusted Book Values	1932	1982
Book value	81.8	881.5	Replacement value	65.4	1,498.6
Index price	64.6	884.4	Index price	64.6	884.4
Price/book value	0.79	1.0	Price/replacement book value	0.99	0.59

There are a couple of important lessons in this table. The first and most pragmatic lesson for the bargain hunter is that one always should be an active interpreter of financial ratios. The casual observer could have discovered easily that the price/book ratio for the Dow Jones Industrial Average in late 1982 was approximately 1.0, and of course

this is a low ratio in a historical context. However, only an active interpreter of the numbers would have taken the time to process intellec-
tually the fact that the historical costs of assets listed on the balance
sheet carried values that were far understated in relation to current
prices. As a brief aside, this adjustment of prices for inflation is called
calculating prices in *real* terms versus *nominal* terms. Economists are
always concerned with the real prices of assets as opposed to their
nominal prices. The practice of looking deeper into the numbers goes
back to our lesson about Uncle John's doctrine of the extra ounce.
Only bargain hunters willing to put in extra work and extra thought
would have uncovered the notion that stocks had never been cheaper
in the U.S. market when viewed in terms of their replacement value.

In a similar vein, there is a parallel between this replacement value
analysis and the analysis that Uncle John used to uncover the hidden
value in the Japanese market that was discussed in Chapter 4. In the
instance of Japan, Uncle John made adjustments to the earnings of
Japanese companies to account for the unreported earnings of the subsidiary companies held by a parent company. In this case, Uncle John
uncovered hidden value by adjusting the asset values of U.S. companies to their market values. In both cases, Uncle John exploited an
inefficiency in information that was not seen by casual observers.

Also, in both cases, Uncle John applied this reasoning in a quest to
get to the truth. In this case, the truth is the answer to the question
"What is the true value of these assets?" When this question was asked
up front, at the beginning of the analytical process, it became common sense to make the adjustments he did and uncover the hidden
value masked by accounting conventions. Casual observers tend to
gloss over accounting treatments and often are led astray by the way
business activity is recorded. Bargain hunters are active interpreters of

the data and dig deeper to interpret accurately what is being presented to them in accounting terms and then compare and contrast the data with what they see as the real-world economic reality of the situation. In the real world, the Japanese companies owned subsidiaries that generated earnings that were not reported in the financial statements. In the real world, the U.S. companies owned assets worth more than the values recorded in the financial statements suggested. In 1982 Uncle John remarked that investors who always talked about the bargains found at the bottom of the market in 1932 were completely unaware of the fact that the market was a much better bargain 50 years later in 1982. Remaining in a constant search for the best bargains in the market prevents the bargain hunter from missing opportunities such as the U.S. market in 1982.

Finally, returning to our original mission of adopting many yardsticks of value, we can see the obvious benefits of judging stocks on more than just one measure, such as a P/E ratio. Stocks appeared to be bargains on a P/E basis, but they were screaming bargains on the basis of the ratio of price to replacement value. In fact, U.S. stocks had never been cheaper and therefore had never represented such an investment opportunity. Even though the P/E ratios and the ratios of price to replacement cost on the Dow Jones should have been enough to have bargain hunters jumping out of their skins to buy U.S. stocks, there were even more clues in the market that stocks were cheap.

Another clue that Uncle John found compelling was the large number of corporate takeovers occurring at that time. One of Uncle John's key recommendations to bargain hunters who are researching a company is to spend nearly as much time researching the company's competitors as they do researching the company itself. Uncle John always said that the best information on any company often came from competitors rather than the company under consideration. The reason for this is that good companies focus on the companies they compete with and spend a great deal of effort trying to stay ahead of their competition. Because of that effort, competing companies over time accumulate a good working knowledge of their competitors as well as the advantages and disadvantages their competitors possess. They also can size up the business environment more quickly than the average bargain hunter can and realize when temporarily unfavorable conditions drive down the market value of a company to a depressed level. Taking all this into consideration, a company's competitors are often on the lookout to absorb capable competitors into their own businesses. The underlying reasons can vary with the circumstances, but typically this is done to adopt the competitor's advantages as their own and eliminate weaknesses.

Thus, when Uncle John observed that the number of companies being taken over was beginning to accelerate, he took this as a market signal, in addition to the others he had observed, that stock prices were far too low relative to the intrinsic values of the companies. Uncle John became even more encouraged that the market was full of bargains when he saw that the prices competitors were willing to pay for those companies ranged from 50 percent to 100 percent above the market value of the target's stock price. This observation can translate into an everyday bargain-hunting strategy. Many astute bargain hunters keep an active watch on the market values of companies whose value becomes too low relative to historical takeover levels in the industry. The most common way bargain hunters detect these relationships is by examining the "enterprise value" of a stock relative to its earnings calculated before interest, depreciation charges, and tax charges (commonly called EBITDA, an acronym for earnings before interest, taxes, depreciation, and amortization). The enterprise value of a firm is simply the stock market equity value of the company plus the amount of debt the company has minus the amount of cash the company carries on the balance sheet. The idea behind the ratio in this use is to get an idea of what a company would cost to purchase in its entirety, since you would have to purchase the equity from the shareholders and assume the company's debt or pay it off.

Enterprise value = equity market value (market cap) + total debt − cash

The point in this calculation is to get a thumbnail sketch of what the takeover value of a company is relative to its "cashlike" earnings. We say that EBITDA is "cashlike" because it often is used as a proxy for cash earnings, but it has some obvious blind spots. In a working example, if we divide the enterprise value of our company by its EBITDA and find that the company's enterprise value is 3 times its EBITDA and we have observed competitors in the industry buying other companies for 6 times their EBITDA, we may be able to conclude that the stock is a bargain on this basis. The underlying rationale is that someone in the market will recognize the stock as a bargain, whether it is a bargain hunter buying the stock or a competitor buying up the company as an acquisition. Returning to the case of the early 1980s, Uncle John's observation that companies were purchasing their competitors for 50 to 100 percent more than their stock prices became a very logical "yardstick of value" measure in addition to the many others he was accumulating at the time.

Yet another thing that Uncle John saw in the market of the early 1980s that suggested that stocks were good bargains was the surging amount of companies that were purchasing their own shares with cash generated from operating their businesses. This activity was compelling to Uncle John because he saw hundreds of companies buying up their shares on the open market because of their depressed levels. Uncle John reasoned that companies purchasing their own shares provided good confirmation that share prices had fallen too low relative to the worth of the companies, because after all, the operators of a company should know its value better than any outside observer. As the companies bought their shares from the market and retired them, this also served to raise the earnings per share of the companies since the shares outstanding were lower relative to the same earnings, all things equal. Many shareholders prefer this activity by the company because it serves to increase EPS and perhaps to raise the value of the company. Many shareholder activists encourage this activity if the company has an increasing amount of cash or a poor record of making new investments in the business with its excess cash. Other investors prefer share repurchase to dividends because receiving a dividend payment also creates a taxable event, and some of the money is wasted through this method of returning money to the shareholder in the form of tax payments to the government.

The last clue that Uncle John offered that prices had become far too low in the stock market and that the trend could reverse was that he observed an overwhelming amount of cash sitting on the sidelines. Uncle John said at the time, "There is more cash available now than I have ever seen in my life." His observation included the large institutional buyers of stocks such as the insurance companies, foreign investors whose own stock markets were trading at levels far above the levels in the United States, and pension funds. At the time, Uncle John saw that U.S. pension funds held about $600 billion. At the same time pension fund experts forecast that the amount of money held by pension funds would reach $3 trillion over the next 12 years. This meant the amount of future money they had to invest eventually would be five times higher. If the pension funds invested at least 50 percent in common stocks (the average has been 55 percent), this suggested that an additional $1.5 trillion *could* come into the stock market. Incidentally, the entire stock market value in 1982 was $1.25 trillion.

This line of reasoning also suggested that there was a good possibility that stock prices would rise on the back of additional buying, simply because the money had to flow somewhere. This contrasts with the more conventional thinking that stock prices would rise on the basis of buying resulting from better earnings and higher intrinsic values. At any rate, Uncle John did not believe stock prices would double on the basis of these pension flows, but he did acknowledge it as one more reason to think that stocks were a good bargain in the United States. All this cash, of course, collates well with the "death of equities" thesis that stated that those institutional buyers might not return to the stock market and would favor real estate, commodities, and collectibles instead of stocks for the rest of time.

Most investors can see the superficial absurdity of this idea, when they contemplate the notion of people's retirement funds or insurance premiums being invested in collectibles such as stamps. However, those commodity and collectible investments were popular at the time, and stocks were not. At that time, no one saw an end to the rampant inflation, the fantastic returns generated by collectibles, or the miserable cloud that hung over the stock market—except at least one investor.

In 1982, Uncle John made an appearance on the popular investing television show hosted by Louis Rukeyser called *Wall Street Week*.

On the show, in the middle of all the pessimism surrounding the U.S. economy and its stock market because of inflation, unemployment, high interest rates, and recession, Uncle John took the consensus view and dashed some cold water in its face. At that time, there were still prevalent views that high inflation and interest rates in the middle to high teens would depress stock P/E ratios permanently at their levels in the low to middle single digits. Uncle John, however, saw the glass as half full and knew from his bargain hunter perspective that stock prices had fallen far too low relative to the value of the businesses they represented. Applying his arsenal of value-measuring yardsticks we have touched on throughout this chapter, he had a strong conviction that the stock market was not dying. On the contrary, he saw a market about to be reborn. Uncle John said that investors were standing on the verge of a great bull market in which the price of the Dow would reach 3,000 over the coming 10 years.

To place this forecast in context, the Dow was trading in the middle to low 800s at the time, and so he was forecasting that the index would increase its value nearly *four times* from its current level over the next 10 years. This was an incredibly bold statement at the time. Onlookers and other market watchers thought he had lost his mind. On the surface, that prediction might have seemed fanciful at the time, but he believed that the prices in the U.S. market represented the best bargains he had seen in his *lifetime,* and he backed his prediction with some commonsense explanations and simple arithmetic.

Uncle John said that if corporate profits grew at their long-term average growth rate of about 7 percent and inflation remained at an expected run rate of around 6 to 7 percent, overall profits would increase approximately 14 percent a year. If those 14 percent gains compounded annually, the values of the stocks would nearly double over the next five years, and if that held up, they would double again in the next five. This corporate earning activity alone would not require the stock market to assign a higher P/E multiple in order to double. However, with the Dow's P/E ratio at around 7× compared with the long-term average of 14×, it was reasonable to see the index getting a lift from a return to the average P/E ratio as well. Then, with all the money sitting on the sidelines and not being invested by institutional buyers, he believed that there was latent firepower to be deployed that would help drive the index higher. In sum, with the environment as poor as it was and all the bad news priced into stocks, the probabilities of conditions improving were very much in his favor as well as the favor of all those holding U.S. stocks. In the nine years that followed, his prediction proved correct.

As Figure 5.2 shows, Uncle John's prediction came to fruition in 1991, and as a result he gained even wider recognition as an authority on investing. What we have to go back to, however, was his willingness to walk into a situation that had been deemed hopeless by all others, examine it with an open mind, and then have the conviction to follow through on his findings and go against the crowd. This practice of looking for bargains where others refuse to look and then having the strength to stand alone on an island is a basic recipe for sustained success in value investing.

Just as Uncle John pointed out that investors who longed for the buying opportunity of 1932 totally missed out on the stock market of the early 1980s, it is important to adopt a mentality that you will examine stocks that others will not, whether an individual instance or an entire country's market full of stocks. For some reason, even those who get the idea that when stocks are depressed it is the correct time to buy still resist doing so. It is an age-old phenomenon, and a perverse one

Figure 5.2

The Dow Jones Industrial Average, 1980–1992

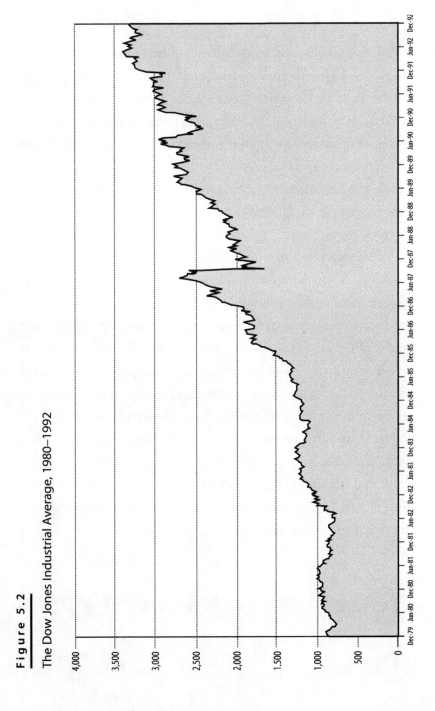

at that, that when stocks go on sale, no one will buy them. Can you imagine teenage girls fleeing a mall, in fact pushing each other out of the way to do so, just as the shops announce that everything is being marked down 50 percent? Of course not; in fact, that would create the opposite experience. Yet this is exactly what happens in the stock market when stocks go on sale.

The way to overcome this human handicap is to rely on quantitative reasoning versus qualitative reasoning. Uncle John always told us that he was quantitative in practice and "never liked a company, only stocks." If your investing methodology is based primarily on calculating the value of a company and looking for prices that are lowest in relation to that value, you would not miss the opportunity found in the death of equities market. However, if you take your cue only from market observers, newspapers, or friends, you will be dissuaded from investing in stocks where the outlook is not favorable. In contrast, if you are independent-minded and focus primarily on numbers versus public opinion, you can create a virtuous investment strategy that will endure in all market conditions. Put another way, if you are finding stocks that are trading at their all-time lows relative to their estimated worth and you find that all other investors have quit the market for those stocks, you are exploiting the point of maximum pessimism, which is the best time to invest.

Chapter | 6

NO TROUBLE TO SHORT
THE BUBBLE

*The four most expensive words in the English language are
"this time it's different."*
—Sir John Templeton

In early 1999 I had just entered the financial world fresh out of
college with an entry-level position in the Atlanta, Georgia, office
of Morgan Stanley Dean Witter. Although I had been an investor
since I was eight years old, beginning with a stock certificate for The
Gap hanging on my bedroom wall, nothing had prepared me for
the stock market of the go-go late 1990s. I was young, and it was eye-
opening to see the excesses from hot technology initial public offer-
ings (IPOs) flowing into the wallets of investment bankers, brokers,
and of course the business casual twenty-somethings running the
companies that were shaping "the new economy."

I could not have chosen a better time to enter the industry,
because observing firsthand the peak euphoria of that market in
2000 followed by the desperate sellers left in its wake packed a lifetime of investing experience into a few years. Also, launching a

hedge fund in the summer of 2001 was quite a market on which to cut one's teeth. This chapter takes us back to the heady days of 1999 and 2000 and begins with a visit my father and I made in early 1999 to Uncle John's house in the Bahamas.

My father and I had just arrived in Nassau, Bahamas, that morning and were sitting down to lunch with Uncle John at the poolside dining area at the Lyford Cay Club where he lives. Not quite sure what to say, I blurted out a largely spontaneous and regrettable question: "Uncle John, have you been buying any technology stocks?" He calmly glanced over at me, gently set his Coke down onto the table, and with the slightest smile said, "Let me tell you a story."

> When I was a young boy growing up in Winchester, Tennessee, I can remember one summer evening at dusk when my brother and I raced down the street on foot to a large crowd gathered outside the front porch of a house. Nearly the whole town was standing outside this man's house, waiting anxiously. Finally, the man appeared at the front door, smiling, and motioned to all of us to wait just a moment. He returned inside the house, and within a moment the whole house lit up with the flip of a switch. The crowd that had gathered yelled and clapped with joy . . . it was the spread of electricity, and it changed the world forever, but the time to get out of those stocks was many years before.

From there he described a number of financial market bubbles that spanned centuries, going back to tulips in Holland in the 1630s. There was a Mississippi bubble conceived by French speculators, a South Sea bubble in England, and of course a railroad boom and bust. Even in more modern times there have been speculative bubbles in wireless radio communication, cars, and televisions. Uncle John has always been fascinated by this behavior, even to the point of having the Templeton Foundation Press issue a reprint of *Extraordinary Popular Delusions and the Madness of Crowds*. What I found most remarkable about his recounting of economic activity that morphs into public euphoria were the common threads of economic circumstances and human behavior in each instance. When you take the time to study the events, even the ones going back centuries, there are familiar elements in each one. If you remember the Internet bubble, you probably have a rough sense of déjà vu when you examine the South Sea bubble in spite of the fact that it occurred in eighteenth-century England.

Take the automobile industry. In its nascent stages during the early 1900s there were few barriers to entry in the business. Just as the late 1990s and 2000 displayed a virtual explosion of dot-com companies, the early commercialization of the automobile in the United States in the period 1900–1908 brought a flurry of 500 automobile manufacturers into the industry. The early automobile producers were really assemblers of parts rather than large-scale manufacturers, just as many early dot-coms simply had an idea and could build a Web site. In either case it did not require much capital to start up a business. Similarly, the public did not seem to contemplate the fate of the initially large number of players, and only the sheer force of competition eventually separated the winners from the losers.

This stands to reason, because the public usually grossly overestimates the industry at the outset. In both industries whose booms and manias were separated by nearly 100 years, the large number of original players shrank dramatically after the busts. Once competition forced the companies to survive on their own ability to make money rather than by raising money from investors, the party ended for the ones just along for the ride. For every General Motors there are several New Era Motors Inc., and for every eBay there are several Webvans. During the building mania phases when the public joins the fray, its willingness to support anything attached to the new industry is maximized. In turn, investors often supply capital to even the most suspect newly hatched operators. Those operators go belly-up when they are no longer supplied with capital, and the naive investors who backed them lose tremendous sums.

Another common thread in every stock mania is the outward display of optimism, with little regard for downside risk. Typically, this optimism is buoyed by outrageous projections of growth for the industry. Also, that growth is perceived to develop in a straight-line fashion without significant disruption. When the automobile industry started a period of rapid growth during the 1910s, the unbridled optimism of endless growth was embraced as a simple *fact*. Coinciding with this notion of endless growth was a latent assumption that there would not be a disruption in the growth; instead, it would continue in a straight-line fashion.

Much like the new economy that was ushered in by the Internet, the advance of the automobile brought us into a "new age." The new age being proclaimed by investors was the age of rapid transportation. From this we can see that technology bubbles, whether in the twentieth or the twenty-first century, always seem to trumpet the concept of a "new age," whether the new economy of the late 1990s–2000 or the age of rapid transit in the 1910s. The similarities between the two bubble periods are clear when we examine newspaper reports from the respective periods. In this excerpt from the *New York Times* in 1912, we can see the implied projections of uninterrupted growth and the idea of entering a new age, in this case one of rapid transit.

> There are many who thoughtlessly look upon the motor car as a fad or craze. Nothing could be farther from the truth, for it must be realized by all that this is the age of rapid transit and the practical need for motor cars is so great and so universal that it is inconceivable that there can be a lessening in the demand.

"Inconceivable that there can be a lessening in the demand." If this is not a one-sided view, what is? Consider this comment in late 1999 from *Wired* magazine. The following excerpt comes from an interview with George Gilder, a technology bull who publishes newsletters on the industry. In this quote we can see once again the underlying assumption of fantastic growth that will come fast and without pause.

> I don't think internet valuations are crazy, I think they reflect a fundamental embrace of huge opportunities. Virtually all forecasts estimate something like a thousand fold rise in internet traffic over the next five years. That means that if you are an internet company today, you are dealing with only a tenth of one percent of your potential traffic in just a couple of years. In ten years at this rate, there would be a million fold increase.

"Millionfold increase"—that is unbridled optimism! To be fair, the automobile and the Internet both changed the world forever. However, we are bargain hunters and are concerned with the fact that they were tremendously overvalued and risky investments once the entire stock market agreed with these opinions in unison and inflated a bubble. Remember the first rule in bargain hunting for stocks: Distinguish between the stock price and the company the stock represents. In this case speculators took the bright idea and bought it regardless of the stock price. The stock price was irrelevant except that it was assumed it would continue to go higher because those companies were changing the world and nothing could stop their growth. Speculators are always drawn into these investments because of the allure of the *idea* and the growth that is sure to follow. As the automobile frenzy ensued in the years that followed, it became clear that the stock market had fallen under its spell of endless growth and profits. The report of trading on Wall Street in 1916 excerpted below captures the mood in the stock market that resulted from unchecked assumptions about the automobile industry's growth.

> There can be no doubt about the automobile craze to one who loiters a while in the brokerage offices these days. The speculator who has just made a "turn" in the auto stocks and doesn't own a motor car is preparing to buy one with his profits, and the equally successful trader with a car is laying his plans to buy a bigger one.

One characteristic that accompanies speculative manias is a wealth-consumption effect. This effect results from the sense of newfound (and lasting) wealth. This psychological shift creates a new compulsion in successful speculators to spend their new wealth. In this case, the stockbrokers who were speculating successfully in auto stocks would use their winnings to purchase new cars. During the Internet bubble of the late 1990s the allure of new wealth affected on day traders and people who started playing Internet stocks as a hobby only to get consumed by the mania. Many day traders committed the cardinal sin of confusing a bull market with genius and quit their jobs to trade full-time. Their plan of course was to keep making money in the stock market and let those gains feed a new level of financial success and personal consumption. In the following excerpt we find a similar instance of new-found wealth and increased consumption in a fourth grade school teacher who had taken up day trading and was profiled in *The Wall Street Journal* in 1999.

> A fourth-grade teacher from Bloomfield Hills, Mich., made a tidy profit buying initial public offerings at their offer prices through accounts at Wit Capital and E*Trade and selling them relatively soon after.
>
> His trading portfolio has swelled to roughly $90,000 from around $2,000, thanks to short-lived investments in hot initial public stock offerings, including Priceline.com and webmethods. He's taking his family to Maui for Easter and was able to buy a DVD player and start some needed repairs on his house.

The auto stock traders bought cars with their winnings in the early 1900s, and the day traders of the 1990s took nice trips and bought electronics. Different time, same story. This behavior can lead to disastrous consequences when the speculators become more aggressive in spending their assumed wealth, which can be gone before the end of the trading day. Similarly, when a large part of the public connects consumption patterns with a forecast of increasing stock prices, it can have negative consequences for the economy when stock prices collapse and spending falls. When higher stock prices propel higher spending over an extended period, the resulting fallout is devastating. These dynamics accompanied the U.S. stock market crash of 1929 as well as the crash of the Japanese stock market and real estate bubble in 1989. This connection between consumption and higher stock prices was also part of the economic paradigm that unraveled during the South Sea bubble in England in 1720.

The South Sea bubble gained notoriety in the eighteenth century and ever since for enticing members from every walk of life. What distinguished this stock mania from most others was the dramatic compression of an entire bubble into a few months' time, whereas many others were built over years. The South Sea bubble occurred when the British parliament struck a deal with the South Sea Company, a merchant shipping vessel company. The deal was for the South Sea Company to assume a large portion of England's debt, which the government would secure (essentially back) by giving South Sea a monopoly on trade in the Spanish Americas. The previous holders of the government debt were offered shares in the South Sea Company that would pay a 6 percent dividend in perpetuity. Also, the holders of the stock stood to gain from any increase in the market value of the shares. Not long after the first deal was struck, the king of England addressed the nation and talked about his desire to reduce the national debt.

Seizing the opportunity, the South Sea operators quickly devised a plan to retire all of England's debt in a similar fashion with the sale of equity. Once the deal was approved and the stock was sold, visions of endless mines of gold and silver in South America and the riches that would accrue took hold of the public imagination. Moreover, the directors of the company pushed those rumors to raise the stock price. The draw of riches from the New World was too much to resist, and the English public became consumed with trading South Sea stock. Observers who were befuddled by the day traders of the late 1990s would have been equally floored by the maverick day traders of South Sea stock in 1720. Day traders have been an ongoing fixture in bubbles dating back at least to eighteenth-century England. In every instance, their willingness to leave all their worldly duties behind in exchange for stock market riches has been unquenchable. The following account, taken from the *Pall Mall Gazette* and personal letters from 1720, makes it easy to imagine how the South Sea stock mania attracted unsuspecting marks from all walks of life.

> Landlords sold their ancestral estates; clergymen, philosophers, professors, dissenting ministers, men of fashion, poor widows, as well as the usual speculators on 'Change, flung all their possessions into the new stock.

The South Sea bubble, much like the Internet bubble, enticed all members of society. The simple fact is that the attraction of easy wealth to a human is unbounded by time or geography. No member of society is exempt. Even the best minds of the time fall prey to it; Sir Isaac Newton lost substantially in the bubble. A noble widow writing a relative from London had the following to say about her experience with the stock of the South Sea Company:

> South Sea is all the talke and fashion; the ladys sell their jewells to bye, and hapy are they that are in. Jemy so pleased with his good fortune, his grave face turn'd to a smiling; he can't looke on you without a simper. Mr. Whitworth gave me 200 guineas for the refusal of South Sea at 500 in two months for 1,000 stocke, I am afraid he will not take it, and I be a rich widow at last. Never was such a time to get money as now.

One of the lady's relatives also corresponded on the events of the day, including speculation. He too was feeling the largesse of easy profits in the market.

> I grow rich so fast I like stock jobbing of all things. Since the South Sea have declared what they give to the annuitants stock has risen vastly. South Sea has this day been 460; they offer 50 per cent for the refusal at 450 for the opening. I think it will be 500 before the shutting.

During the South Sea bubble and most of the manias that followed, there were good examples of the public's distaste for naysayers who spoke against the mania. In 1720 a wise financier and former chancellor of the exchequer named Robert Walpole objected to the creation of the South Sea stock and was outspoken in his disapproval of the project. His argument against the South Sea stock's creation is excerpted below.

> The dangerous practice of stockjobbing would divert the genius of the nation from trade and industry. It would hold out a dangerous lure to decoy the unwary to their ruin by making them part with the earnings of their labor for a prospect of imaginary wealth. The great principle of the project was an evil of first-rate magnitude; it was to raise artificially the value of the stock by exciting and keeping up a general infatuation and by promising dividends out of funds which could never be adequate for the purpose.

Walpole was right on the money. He spoke of the unsuspecting day traders who would get dragged into the game before it even got started. His concerns and warnings were dismissed as a distraction. There is a lesson in this event that basically says that anyone who stands in the way of the conventional wisdom supporting a mania will get bowled over by the masses. This was equally true during the dot-com frenzy, when day traders were glorified for their big winnings and old guard bargain hunters were publicly chided for not participating in the big gains. Most noticeable is the exaggerated confidence of the speculators as the mania gains steam and heightens their hubris.

During the dot-com mania two particularly successful value investors, Julian Robertson and Warren Buffett, seemed to catch more than their fair share of public criticism for not purchasing shares of inflated technology stocks and thus underperforming the market. On December 27, 1999, the financial publication *Barron's* ran a cover story titled "What's Wrong, Warren?" The article addressed Buffett's lagging returns in the 1999 market and suggested that he had been left behind by a new type of investor:

> But there's more to Berkshire's weak showing than just the operating and investment performance. To be blunt, Buffett, who turns 70 in 2000, is viewed by an increasing number of investors as too conservative, even passe.

This article, like the death of equities piece from 1979, is viewed in hindsight as a joke, but it was no joke at the time. The published financial pundits and masses of day traders were lining up to ridicule long-standing bargain hunters and revel in their underperformance. Nothing quite captures the moment like another article run in *The Wall Street Journal* in December 1999. In this article, a social worker turned day trader has her stock-trading prowess pitted against Buffett's.

A social worker in Redondo Beach, Calif., had never bought a single share of stock. She didn't think the market was for her. "I didn't understand it," she confesses. Then, while driving one day, she heard on the radio that a local company "had signed a contract with Russia that sounded interesting." After calling for more information, she set up her first brokerage account and bought 100 shares at $12 each. Today, that company is MCI WorldCom Inc. Her original $1,200 now is worth $16,000, part of a mid-six-figure portfolio that includes Red Hat Inc., Yahoo! Inc., General Electric Co. and America Online Inc.

"I've doubled my money in two years, I'm staggered, aren't you? It's amazing. You can't make that in social work."

Along with Wall Street's heavy hitters, Main Street investors have emerged as a powerful financial force in the 1990s, simultaneously boosting their net worths beyond their wildest dreams and helping to propel the market to records. Indeed, individual investors now account for more than 30% of the New York Stock Exchange's trading volume, up from less than 15% in 1989. Walk into any workplace—not just office buildings, but auto dealerships, taverns and factories—and there's a good chance people will be bantering about investments.

Her stock picking has been so successful that she's cut back her social work to weekends and spends weekdays trading full-time from home. "I make a few buys and a few sells each day," she says. Her goal: to make $150,000 in annual trading profits to build a financial cushion that she and her husband can live on in retirement.

Along the way, she has developed a few investing philosophies that speak volumes about how deeply ingrained "momentum" investing has become—and how utterly unfashionable it is to focus on "value" stocks. "All these people say 'buy and hold,'" she says. "If a stock continues to decline, there comes a time when you better get off the boat."

The lesson? "You have to sell your losers. If a stock goes up, it's not because I was a whiz. And if the tape goes against me," she adds, "I won't stick around. I keep my losses to 10%."

Take that, Warren Buffett.

"Take that, Warren Buffett"? They sure did go after the poor guy, most likely because of his long-standing successful use of value investing. By the way, MCI WorldCom played a shell game of accounting fraud that a few years later made history as the largest bankruptcy in the United States. This is another illustration of the endless confidence that day traders had in their technology stocks. Their stock selection methods were based on momentum trading, which, reduced to its simplest method, means that you buy things that are going up and sell things that are going down. In other words, the entire game plan is to follow the herd. This undying confidence in tech stocks signaled to experienced bargain hunters that the house of cards was about to fall.

The example of MCI WorldCom during the technology bubble provides another powerful illustration of the timeless links between human behavior and stock manias. One of the unfortunate features of asset bubbles is the unscrupulous figures that emerge to cash in on the unsuspecting public. MCI WorldCom was a behemoth of a telecommunications company that rode the wave of technology share prices into one acquisition after another. The company was pieced together in a series of acquisitions throughout the late 1990s under the auspice of its now infamous (and imprisoned) CEO,

Bernie Ebbers. The company's plan was simple: It was consolidating the telecommunications industry by using its inflated share price as a currency to buy out competitors. The company's crowning achievement would have been its acquisition of Sprint for $115 billion, but antitrust regulators blocked the deal. Not long after this letdown, the entire technology bubble fell apart and Ebbers began to feel the heat in his personal investments, which were funded through $400 million worth of loans collateralized by his stock in MCI WorldCom. If that stock had continued to fall, he would have been in way over his head without collateral for his massive borrowing.

When MCI WorldCom stock began to fall because of pressure from the Internet bust, he manipulated the share price of his holdings by initiating accounting fraud that would mask the declining conditions of the business and fool the stock market into keeping the share price high. Before that point the company had been reporting growth and higher earnings through all the businesses it had been tacking on through acquisitions, but once the acquisitions dried up after the failure of the Sprint purchase, there were no more easy accounting levers to pull to report higher earnings. After Arthur Andersen was replaced as auditor by KPMG, the fraudulent accounting came to light in the audit process and Ebbers's goose was cooked. In the end, investors lost $180 billion. This was a scheme for the ages, one that would have made Abe White proud. Who is Abe White? you ask.

In the wireless bubble, that is, the wireless telegraph bubble of 1904, we see another example of the public being led along a path to fool's gold. During that early twentieth-century technology bubble the wireless telegraph form of communication (radio messages) captured the imagination and of course the wallets of the American public. It began with the Marconi system of wireless telegraphy and ended with copycats trying to cash in on the mania.

Guglielmo Marconi was an Irish-Italian born into a well-established family of distillers (Jameson) and real estate owners. His mother had him tutored in physics by a professor in Bologna who happened to be experimenting with the transmission of signals on the same frequency between transmitters and receivers. Through careful study and perseverance Marconi was able to combine advances in telephony and the study of electromagnetic waves into the wireless transmission of messages.

Although similar experiments were being conducted in academic circles, Marconi was a capitalist at heart and sought commercial applications. After additional research, the filing of patents, and a successful demonstration of his system for the Italian Navy, he incorporated his work into a business financially backed by a cousin. Not long afterward, the Marconi Wireless Telegraph Company was born. Riding on the example of Edison to gain further financial backing for a new technology, Marconi staged public demonstrations of his technology. He sent a message across the English Channel to France and broadcast the results of the America's Cup yacht race to the Associated Press. Through the support of newspapers and those promotions, Marconi was causing quite a stir, but the technology, like all new technologies, had limitations. In this case, messages were restricted to about 35 miles.

The promotional events did not go unnoticed and attracted the attention of would-be competitors ready to break into the game, commercialize the technology, and become rich. One such rival was Lee De Forest, a young Yale Ph.D. who, backed by classmates, formed the Wireless Telegraph Company of America. The company tried to stage a coming-out party by broadcasting the 1901 America's Cup race (two years after Marconi's original broadcast) to the Publisher's Press Association while Marconi broadcast to the Associated Press. Both were using the same frequency, which made the airwaves a bit jammed with interference. Also, there was a third wireless company, the American Wireless Telephone and Telegraph Company, that was deeply frustrated that it could not obtain a press publication to relay its own broadcast of the race. In their frustration, they found a nearby island and perched there hidden during the race to run a broadcast of nonsense and obscenity (directed at Marconi and De Forest, no less) with the sole intent of sabotaging their two competitors. Observers of the race and the broadcast said that what little could be understood over the airwaves was not fit to print.

With Marconi as the basic leader of the industry in both technology and stature, De Forest needed to raise more capital and decided to do that in a hurry. Although he initially was successful in raising more money, his efforts stalled within a year until he attracted the attention of a man named Abraham White. White gained notoriety on Wall Street for obtaining a "postage stamp bid" for an issue of bonds quoted at $1.5 million in 1796 that transformed him from rags to riches. White had shopped an issue of bonds from Washington around Wall Street and in doing so received quotes from a number of investors. He then mailed in a series of bids to Washington, D.C., for the bonds and, in the absence of a required deposit, won the bid. White promptly took the offer, found a financial backer for the deposit, and sold the bonds he obtained for $1.5 million at a premium on Wall Street. That was a conspicuous beginning on Wall Street for someone with a gift for stock promotion. White teamed up with De Forest, assuming the position of president while De Forest became vice president.

White's tactics as president can best be described as promotion on steroids with the intent of raising as much money as possible from the public. There were publicity stunts such as fastening a wireless tower to a car and parking it on Wall Street, and they constructed a useless wireless tower in Atlanta to gain public attention. Before long, White had raised the capital amount to $5 million, or about $116 million in today's dollars. Shortly thereafter he merged the company with the International Wireless Company, the group of equally shady characters that had sabotaged the America's Cup broadcasts. Reportedly, the International Wireless Company, once the American Wireless Telephone and Telegraph Company, had been transformed under a string of acquisitions consisting of suspect stock-jobbing operators. The combined company was thought to be worth $15 million ($350 million in 2006 dollars).

The main goal was to sell worthless paper to the public, particularly once White gained full control and pushed De Forest out. De Forest was hardly an innocent in the scheme, as evidenced by his diaries: "Soon we believe the suckers will begin to bite." After being pushed out by White, he fled the country for selling patent-infringing equipment to the U.S. Navy. White then kicked into overdrive a barrage of tactics aimed at inflating the company's stock. Phony financial reports were released to the press, promising prospectuses were sent to investors, and there were carnival-like publicity stunts. In one public speech, White's empty promise to the public went like this:

A few hundred dollars invested in De Forest stock now will make you independent for life. Tremendous developments are under way. Just as soon as the company is on a dividend basis the stock should advance to figures practically without limit. If set aside for two years it is morally certain to be in demand at 1,000 percent or more present prices. Those who buy will receive returns little less than marvelous. A hundred dollars put into this stock now for your children will make them independently rich when they reach their majority.

The money that came in from share sales to the public was listed later in the financial statements as revenue, and so the only way to increase revenue was to sell more shares. Once share sales stalled, so would the entire charade. To prevent share sales from stalling, White poured it on thicker and heavier:

There is not enough stock to go round. Consider the matter carefully. You have the opportunity. Will you grasp it at the flood tide and ride on to the shore of plenty, high and dry above the adversities which often beset old age, to the land of your dreams, where wealth is unbounded and every wish gratified, where comforts admit of enjoyment, and wealth admits of opportunities for yourself and those you love? Or will you hesitate and doubt and let the chance go by, to remain in senile dependency upon the bounty of others? Think! It is for you to decide! Think well! Buy! Do it now!

Not only did he go over the top in his pitches, he took the game to another level in describing the promises of his company's technology. He sent a wire to the White House promising President Roosevelt wireless messages to Manila in 18 months. He promised a San Francisco–New York line. He promised instantaneous messages from the Pacific coast to China. Shortly thereafter White remade his company in a press release proclaiming that the United Wireless Telegraph Company had been formed with the intent to merge all the international concerns, including Marconi's, of the wireless industry into one fold. The Marconi people of course were outraged and in fact already had filed suit against White for patent infringement.

By 1910, Abe White's game was over. The feds raided his offices in New York, citing the reams of literature that had been sent out extolling marvelous growth and an impregnable financial condition. In sum, they were looking for mail fraud on the basis of the deluge of fantastical mailings and solicitations sent from the United Wireless offices. What they found probably surprised them. The feds discovered that the supposed assets of the company of $14 million did not exist; the value of the company's assets was about $400,000. The directors had controlled the stock through a lockup for the public holders by stamping the shares nontransferrable until 1911. In the meantime, the directors kept adjusting the price of the stock upward on the basis of new contracts (which were in fact money-losing) in $5 increments. The stock began selling at $1.50 and was adjusted over time up to $50. In the meantime the directors unloaded their stock on the captive public, who could not sell it, at ever higher prices. This scheme resulted in the fleecing of 28,000 shareholders who had been rabid for wireless company shares. The feds relieved Abe White of his 15 million shares, which, priced at $50 before the raid, had run his personal stake to $750 million in 1910, or $16.2 billion in today's dollars.

The stories of Bernie Ebbers and Abe White unveil the ugly sides of stock manias. Both show how crooks exploited greed among naive speculators and sold them a bag of lies. However, even in the perfectly legal and morally acceptable circumstances surrounding stock manias, investors buy into a constant succession of newly issued stocks at exorbitant prices on the basis of what can only be called naïve misconceptions.

In the large majority of stock manias one can observe new companies that are selling stock to the public for the first time through an initial public offering (IPO). Whenever you observe an IPO in any market condition, bubble or not, your bargain hunter instincts should make you cautious. Do not get caught up in the excitement that is intended to maximize the price of the stock and therefore the amount of money the company will raise from the public. Companies often use IPOs or secondary issues of stock to raise money when they think their ability to do so is maximized. Therefore, they issue stock when they think the price is high. If the price is high, you are not getting a bargain. Pretty simple, right?

In December 1999, an orgy of greed was broadcast over the technology channel of the stock market. Value investors were much too uncool for the party. Value investors looked at P/E ratios, paid attention to cash flows, measured returns on capital, favored stable balance sheets, and probably never had heard of a "cash burn rate" in any medium, much less investment analysis. They cared about the strategy of the business and the experience of the operators. Out with the old, in with the new. The investing heroes of yesterday were brought to their knees.

Perhaps amused by what was occurring in the market at that point, another "old hand" was studying these events carefully, as he always did, and was ready to expose the new age of investing as another familiar story in the history of the markets. The market had become a circus, and it was time to show it the way out of town.

I was at home with my parents for Christmas in 1999 when my father walked into the room and told me he had just received a fax from Uncle John. The fax contained a relatively long list of NASDAQ technology stocks that Uncle John recommended selling short.

Selling short is the popular practice in which an investor bets that a stock will drop in price rather than rise. The goal in selling short is to profit from falling stock prices, as opposed to going long, in which you hope to profit from rising stock prices. You execute this transaction by telling your broker which company's shares you would like to sell short, at which time the broker "borrows" the shares from another holder on your behalf (you do not own the shares). The broker immediately sells the borrowed shares in the market, and your plan as an investor is to purchase the shares after they experience the decline in price you are anticipating.

If the shares decline in price and you buy them back at the lower price, you will make a profit that consists of the difference between the price you initially sell the shares at—let's say $50 a share—and the price you purchase the shares at—let's say $40. Your broker returns the shares to the lender at $40, and you keep the $10 profit, the difference between the initial $50 price and the subsequent price of $40. The idea is to return the shares to the lender at a lower price and reap the benefit of initially selling them at a higher price to yourself. However, if the shares rise in price, you effectively lose money because you will have to repurchase the shares at, say, $60, which means you owe the lender the difference of $10 when you return the shares.

Short selling is not for the meek investor because the most you can make in a short sell is 100 percent. You profit 100 percent when your $50 stock you sold short falls in price to $0. In that case, you return shares to the lender that are worthless and keep the entire $50 profit from selling the shares to yourself.

Let's put the mechanics of the transaction aside and get to the meat of the situation. As you can see, there is no upward boundary on a stock price, and that means your potential for loss is unlimited. Some preventive measures are put in place by the brokerage houses, such as requiring you to post more cash into the account when losses mount, but this is not something to view as a security blanket. It is more akin to a bar cutting off someone who has had too much to drink; when you think about it, that is a bad sign because bars want you to drink. In sum, the relationship between risk and reward can get dangerous very quickly in a short sell transaction. Aspiring short sellers are cautioned to hold dear the words of John Maynard Keynes, a famous economist and an avid and successful investor in his own right: "The market can stay irrational longer than you can stay solvent."

There were many other bargain hunters who attempted to sell short technology shares on the NASDAQ exchange in the years leading up to the crash, but in practice it was more like stepping in front of a bus. In earlier chapters we discussed the importance of avoiding "story stocks," or stocks whose prices have become so disconnected from the economic value of the company that they are hopelessly overpriced and ripe for a fall.

The technology stocks trading on the NASDAQ in the late 1990s should be inducted into the story stock hall of fame. Story stocks typically are backed by some product on which investors become fixated. Some of those stocks did not even have products backing them. These were stocks representing companies that in many cases were not really companies in a traditional sense but were just "business ideas." In the later stages of the market bubble, the crazy prices that speculators paid for those stocks scaled directly with the crazy ideas backing the businesses. Business plans were passé. The best advice a budding entrepreneur could have received in 1999 was to put an *e* in front of a business's name; that was all that was necessary to ensure that it would be a smashing success in the eyes of the speculators funding those start-ups. This was the new economy, and it was changing the world. To be fair, some good, lasting businesses were formed in that era, but there were also a lot of ridiculous, if not fantastical, assumptions driving the prices of those stocks, including the enduring businesses. To put this in perspective the price/earnings ratio on the NASDAQ had climbed to 151.7× by December 1999 (see Figure 6.1). Bargain hunters can see that not only were these story stocks, they were being priced on pure fantasy.

As the surging P/E ratio valuation indicates, the NASDAQ had turned into a runaway train over the course of 1999. This posed a significant problem for bargain hunters who might have gotten the idea to sell those NASDAQ shares short. The problem was that you were dashing into oncoming traffic. That traffic was dense, moving fast and swerving recklessly. It was an interstate highway of lawlessness fueled by the new economy. Bargain hunters unfortunate enough to step into traffic to short those stocks at the wrong time or the wrong location were reduced to road kill. The stocks on the NASDAQ in late 1999 set new record highs on a weekly, if not daily, basis. Stocks went higher because the crowd willed them higher with more buying. Stocks went simply higher because they had gone higher the day before. Neophytes became stock market geniuses after one trade. Day traders were running the show, and the main feature was momentum. It was the only program, and if you did not like it, there was nothing else playing. The concept of valuing a stock or the notion that a stock's prices should be constrained by the company it represented was masked by the party tub of tech Kool-Aid, and too many people were drinking from it.

Figure 6.1

NASDAQ Composite Monthly Price-to-Earnings Ratio, 1995–1999

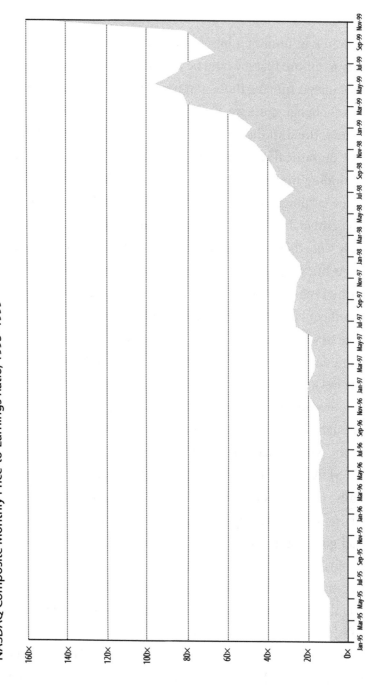

In some of our earlier discussions we talked about the pitfalls of bargain hunting. One of those pitfalls is the common experience of identifying bargains ahead of the crowd and watching the crowd continue to sell your bargain stock down to even lower levels. It is not unusual to invest a little early and feel the pain of watching continued selling in your stock and seeing its price drop.

Let's take this relationship and reverse it. As a bargain hunter equipped with the proper perspective and tools seeking to short sell a stock, chances are that you will sell short too early, before the buying has waned or the current buyers recognize their errors and become sellers. Because of this, short selling on the basis of bargain hunter methods can be frustrating, if not treacherous. Most often, bargain hunters will need to cover their shorts before the pain of losses becomes too much to bear, only to see the stock collapse some time in the future. Unfortunately, there is no consolation prize for a stock falling after you have covered your short and returned the shares; losses are losses.

Every short seller faces this basic peril of short selling too early and facing losses that can come quick and heavy. With this in mind, let us imagine the kind of challenge Uncle John was taking on at the end of 1999 by trying to short stocks in one of the fastest-moving stock markets on record.

If only there was a way to figure out what would spark the selling in those stocks and bring down the biggest charade in the history of twentieth-century markets. There was. Uncle John took a different perspective on this phenomenon to discover a hidden gem in the market and a highly probable approach to generating short sell profits rather than losses. If there is one psychological element present in a stock market bubble, it is greed. It is an old flaw among humans, and it is manifested routinely in the stock market.

Suffice it to say that there were buyers in the market who were eager to cash out their winnings and take the money and run. Who were they? They were the young and old executives of the technology firms that were coming to the stock market in an IPO on a daily basis. It is very common for a company that is entering an initial public offering in the stock market to reward its managers with large allocations of the new stock of the company. This makes sense because they are very often the owners of the company before it is sold to the public through the stock market.

In the IPO market of 1999 and 2000, before the crash, young executives were making wheelbarrows of money by offering the stocks of their companies to the public. It was a lightning-quick way to become a millionaire (on paper at least), and it was based on the stock market's voracious appetite for tech stocks. Therefore, the individuals managing those tech firms had a tremendous incentive to get their firms up and going by calling an investment banker and trying to sell the companies (which sometimes were just an idea for a company) to the public.

If you are not familiar with the IPO market, we may seem to be painting it in a harsh light. To digress for a moment, taking a company public is in normal circumstances an important function of the capital markets because it not only transfers ownership for healthy reasons but usually is necessitated by some desired need for funding at a company. Funding can be sought for any number of reasons but usually has a catalyst such as expanding the business. In exchange for the funding, the owners give up a percentage of ownership to the public shareholders who buy the stock during the

IPO or afterward. Of course, after the IPO, the money changes hands only between the buyers and sellers and does not flow back to the company unless the company decides to offer more stock.

There are a couple of useful observations about IPOs in general that we can make as bargain hunters. The first is that typically managers offer stock to the public when there is great enthusiasm for shares in an absolute sense. It is widely accepted that no one can time the tops and bottoms of stock market runs, but it generally is accepted that a sudden surge in IPOs suggests that a market is inflating because managers and investment bankers try to maximize the amount of money they can raise for a company when they take it public. Coincidentally, their efforts can run in parallel with more expensive market levels or, for that matter, with the later stages of a bull market. The second observation is that when IPOs are made, the enthusiasm for the shares often pushes the offering price above its intrinsic value because of the heavier than normal demand. It is not unusual to see shares fall in price months after an IPO takes place as enthusiasm and demand die down and normalize when the stock is traded freely in the open market.

For these reasons Uncle John rarely participated in the buying of IPO shares even when he managed his mutual funds because he found that he could purchase the shares at a better price months or even years after they initially were offered. In other words, he thought that IPOs are a bad deal if you are looking for a bargain. An old rule of thumb for the majority of investors is that if you can get the shares of an IPO, you probably do not want them, since the hottest IPOs go to the biggest clients.

In the IPO market of 1999 and 2000, the new-issue market was a quick way for business managers to cash out their inflated stakes at the public's expense, and in many cases there were abuses. Uncle John recognized that among all the participants in the technology stock market bubble, those stockholders had the biggest incentive to sell. Those company managers, or "insiders," knew what kind of hand they were holding (a weak one) and were more than ready to cash out and take their winnings early. To be blunt, insiders in those companies were happy to sell to the public their personal slice of the new economy the first chance they got.

Normally, however, after an IPO is conducted and the individuals who are offered shares to purchase in the IPO make their purchases, there is a period when activity among the insiders is prevented by market regulations. In other words, there is typically a six-month period in which insiders must sit quietly and hold their stock before they can sell it. This is commonly referred to as an IPO lockup period. Uncle John researched all the technology IPOs coming to the market and found out when their lockup periods expired, which told him when the insiders could begin selling their personal shares into the market. He was certain that the insiders would sell their shares. He was also certain that insider selling would create the catalyst that was needed to put widespread selling pressure on the stocks. This was necessary because the buyers and sellers of technology stocks at that point were making decisions solely by observing the daily movements in the stock prices of their holdings. In other words, if the day traders saw a stock price going up, they would buy some to get in on the action.

At the same time, technology stocks were being bought and pushed higher on a daily basis. However, if the stock prices started falling, the previous buyers had no other basis for ownership except that the price had been going up. Once the prices started to fall, the holders had little reason to stick around. In sum, the insiders would not be the primary force driving the prices down, but by initiating heavy selling, they would light the fuse that would ignite a chain reaction of selling. That chain reaction would result in a total meltdown in technology shares.

Uncle John devised a strategy to sell short technology shares 11 days or so before the lockup expired in anticipation of heavy selling by insiders once they were allowed to unload their shares on the public. He concentrated on technology issues whose values had increased three times over the initial offering price. He reasoned that stocks that had increased that much in value provided an extra incentive to insiders to cash out and sell their holdings. In sum, he found 84 stocks that met this criterion and decided to place a position of $2.2 million into each short sell.

All told, he bet $185 million of his own money that tech stocks would plummet at the height of the bubble. In the second week of March 2000, plummet they did (see Figure 6.2).

We mentioned earlier that Uncle John was asked during a talk how one could identify the point of maximum pessimism. His response was that when the last holder decides to throw in the towel and sell the stock, all the sellers by definition are gone and buyers are all that can be left. Taking this logic and reversing it for the 2000 technology bubble, the point of maximum optimism was reached when there were no more buyers left in the market, and the sellers were about to take control. That point was reached on March 10, 2000, when the NASDAQ hit its all-time high of 5,132. An article ran that day in *The Wall Street Journal*, as the NASDAQ peaked, that was titled "Conservative Investors Warm Up to Idea That Tech Sector Isn't a Fad." The most unforgiving bargain

Figure 6.2

NASDAQ Composite Index Prices, January–December 2000

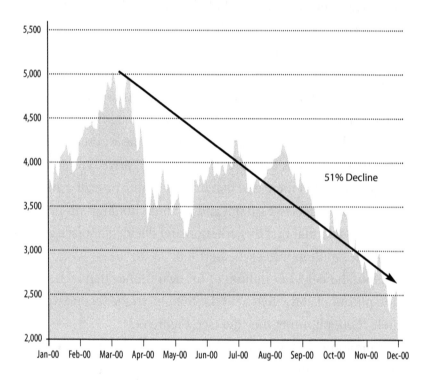

hunters would call this a heavy dose of poetic justice, as the article profiled investors who had been married to conservative investing only to jump ship at the last moment and get into the tech stock casino.

The little light bulb came on last summer. The 41-year-old project manager had been meticulously building a conservative stock portfolio since the mid-1980s strike with solid, safe blue-chip names such as DuPont, Johnson & Johnson and Procter & Gamble. Technology highfliers, anything that traded at more than 30 times earnings, seemed "outlandish," he recalls. Then came his epiphany.

He saw a brand-new software company called Red Hat triple on its first day of trading, one of dozens doing similar things, and he began mentally kicking himself.

"It took me until then to realize that people had changed their mindset," It dawned on him that the economy had shifted, and that companies that made diapers, chemicals and BandAids weren't exactly at the epicenter of the action.

Well, duh, as his kids might put it. He was late to the party, but now he was going to dance.

"I think the Cisco Systems, the Lucents, the Oracles, the World-Coms and the Vodaphones are the core stocks to hold for the future," the once-conservative investor now says. "It's like when the railroads started up and were changing the whole face of the nation. The example I use with my kids is that a year ago, we didn't have a cell phone. Now we have three—four, counting my daughter who just went to college. When I got my M.B.A. in 1994 I had no computer; now I have four."

No plunger, he studied the new stocks carefully, and as the autumn wore on, he began to move. Using the Internet for research, checking chat rooms and message boards that he would have scoffed at in April, he began buying tech stocks, which now account for the bulk of his seven-figure portfolio.

He is one of countless bedrock American investors who have undergone a transformation in recent months. For a long time, they sneered at "new paradigm" talk as a bunch of mumbo jumbo, and decried giddy neophytes loading up on tech stocks as speculators who were sure to get their comeuppance. Now, these conservative investors are feeling stupid—and, worse, the poorer for it. They have started buying tech stocks themselves. This tectonic shift has helped push the Nasdaq Composite Index, the home of the hot tech names, up 100% since August—through 3000 in November, 4000 in December and to its first close above 5000 Thursday. Meanwhile, the Dow Jones Industrial Average, home of P&G, DuPont and Eastman Kodak, has languished, and the Standard & Poor's 500-stock index has posted a comparatively modest gain.

In the course of a few months, many people have changed their definition of a blue-chip stock. Out with shares that had been in portfolios for generations, names such as Coca-Cola, Philip Morris and AT&T. The new blue chips are Cisco, Intel—and even heretofore unknown companies such as fiber-optics highflier JDS Uniphase.

Despite the leftover old-economy stocks his portfolio is up more than 40% since Sept. 1—not as good as a pure tech-stock index, but a lot better than the 8.5% decline that the DJIA has turned in since then.

Others are going a step further. Conservative people, some in their 80s, are walking into their financial advisers' offices and demanding that their mutual funds or their managed portfolios begin to include a piece of the soaring new economy. The more people make the switch, the more the trend snowballs.

That article was run the day the NASDAQ hit its all-time high. As it implies, the very last buyers finally had come into the market. The only remaining holdouts finally cried uncle and dived into the mania. This is the kind of pressure you can expect to feel when your bargain-hunting methods are out of style, as they will be from time to time, and the urge to jump into what is working at the moment grips you like an anaconda. We know from many previous examples that that is exactly the wrong move. What would an article written on the day of the NASDAQ's all-time high be without a few pot-shots at Buffett and Robertson thrown in for good measure?

> He is old economy through and through, and his portfolio is feeling it. At Mr. Buffett's Berkshire Hathaway Inc., five of the largest publicly traded holdings disclosed by the firm are off at least 15% from their highs. Gillette is down 51%, Washington Post is off 19%, Coke is off 47%, American Express has lost 27%, and Freddie Mac is down 42%. Berkshire Hathaway itself, considered by some a stock-market paragon, is down 48%.
>
> Or consider hedge-fund manager Julian Robertson, long seen as one of the smartest men on Wall Street. He has been paid millions to manage money for some of the nation's richest investors, but he hasn't had the light-bulb experience. His Tiger Fund stumbled 19% last year and was down 6% more in January. He made a big, and so far bad, bet on the old economy's US Airways.

Within a year the NASDAQ Index had fallen off a cliff and declined 51 percent from its March peak. As you might have guessed, the dramatic collapse in the index does not do justice to the carnage that unfolded in individual stocks within the composite. Among the technology stocks that Uncle John sold short, there were many that lost 95 percent of their value from the point where he shorted them. To provide just a few illustrations of these positions, Figures 6.3 through 6.5 show the expiration dates of the lockups, the cost basis for the positions, and the profits that followed taking the positions.

Figure 6.3

Stock Price of Breakaway Solution

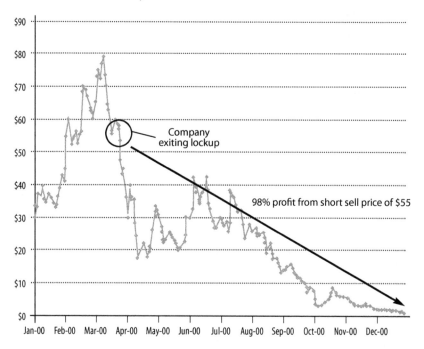

You may have noticed that in some cases, such as Foundry Networks, Uncle John's shorts coincided with the top of the NASDAQ bubble, but some did not, such as the Vyyo short, which was executed in November 2000, well after the initial market crash. This is instructive because it tells us that the path from euphoria to pessimism takes time, at least months but more often years, just as the path from pessimism to euphoria can also take months, if not years.

In this discussion we have covered much detail on the circumstances surrounding these short sells at the height of the NASDAQ bubble but little on the mechanics of the execution. Bargain hunters looking to short outrageously priced securities in the future may benefit from some of the techniques Uncle John employed in his short trades.

The first rule is to control your losses. The second rule is to remember the first rule. To control your losses, it may be wise to set up a list of rules to follow strictly once you have sold your shares short. For example, when Uncle John sold short these shares in the NASDAQ, he established a few rules to guide him through the decision-making process.

The most important rule is to establish a preset level at which you will decide to cut your losses and cover the stock. In the case

Figure 6.4

Stock Price of Foundry Networks

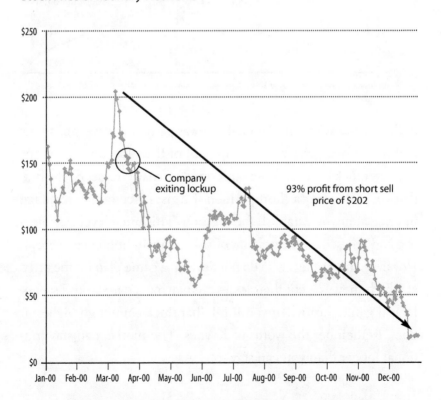

Figure 6.5
_____

Stock Price of Vyyo

of the NASDAQ shorts, Uncle John was particularly wary of shorts that had strong price rises coming out of their lockup expirations and was quick to cover those positions. You may choose to set a rule that you will cover a short position if it rises a certain percentage in price after you establish the position. This price level is subjective and is based on the amount of risk a bargain hunter can accept. However, short sellers who do not develop a game plan for the price at which they will cut their losses are playing a dangerous psychological game. Just when you think that stock cannot go higher, it does. Remember the words of Keynes: The market can stay irrational longer than you can stay solvent.

In the same vein, a bargain hunter should elect to take profits on a predetermined basis. For instance, when Uncle John sold short these NASDAQ shares, he established guidelines for that aspect of the trade also. In this case, he elected to take profits when the stock price lost 95 percent of its value after he sold it short or when the stock fell below a price/earnings ratio of 30× based on trailing 12 months' earnings per share. These rules for taking profits are almost as important as the ones for taking losses as they prevent bargain hunters from reaching too far or becoming greedy. The idea is to take advantage of the greed with a clear and objective mind rather than lose objectivity.

It is not hard to see that greed was one of the key determinants that sparked the rout in NASDAQ shares over the course of 2000. In the first quarter of 2000 alone $78 billion of IPOs were brought to the market, along with $110 billion in recent IPOs freed from their lockup periods. In a sense, the technology bubble crumbled under the weight of its own greed and insiders' attempt to unload shares on the public.

Going back to our discussions of poker, it is clear now that the technology bubble was the biggest bluff of all time. Smart players knew it was a bluff then, but it was a high-stakes game, and at some point they probably decided that it was better to live for another game rather than sit at the table and call the bluff. For old hands, it was just a matter of biding their time; observing the weakness of the players, which was their greed; and then leaving with the pot at the end of the night.

All told, Uncle John pocketed over $90 million doing just that. Take that, day trader!

Chapter | 7

CRISIS EQUALS OPPORTUNITY

When written in Chinese, the word "crisis" is
composed of two characters—one represents danger,
and the other represents opportunity
—John F. Kennedy

There is an old saying in the financial markets that Uncle John has repeated throughout his career: "The best time to buy is when there's blood in the streets." This is not meant to be morbid but refers to the selling in stock markets that follows a crisis that leads to a panic. From a stock market standpoint, the terrorist attacks on September 11, 2001, in New York were no different from dozens of other crisis incidents that have played out over the centuries in the financial markets. The results were similar: panicked selling of shares. When the markets reopened on September 17, 2001, the stock market again played a familiar tune waiting to be heard by bargain hunters with a trained ear.

Uncle John knew very well at that stage in his career how to turn a market panic into future returns and understood that a war-related crisis presented outstanding opportunities for investment. That experience goes far back into his career, including his purchase of securities in 1939 as World War II erupted in Europe. For bargain hunters, it is easy to grasp how promising investing opportunities are when shares are sold aggressively with no regard to their value. Investing on the heels of a crisis, when sellers are scared and driven by fear, represents the best of these opportunities. The opportunities are even greater when the economic consequences are not understood or are overestimated.

One way to think about the strategy of purchasing shares in the wake of a crisis is to relate the current crisis to the same strategies that a bargain hunter employs on a daily basis in common market conditions. First, the bargain hunter searches for stocks that have fallen in price and are priced too low relative to their intrinsic value. Typically, the best opportunities to capture these bargains come during periods of highly volatile stock prices. Second, the bargain hunter searches for situations in which a large misconception has driven stock prices down, such as the arrival of near-term difficulties for a business that are temporary in nature and should correct over time. In other words, bargain hunters look for stocks that have become mispriced as a result of temporary changes in the near-term perspectives of sellers. Third, the bargain hunter always investigates stocks when the outlook is worst according to the market, not best.

A crisis sends all these events into overdrive. Put another way, when the market sells off in a panic or crisis, all the market phenomena a bargain hunter desires condense into a brief and compact period: maybe a day, a few weeks, a few months, perhaps even longer. Typically, though, the events and the reactions to them do not last long. Because of their ability to grip sellers, panics and crises create by far the best opportunities to pick up bargains, which drop into your lap if you have the ability to stay seated while everyone else dashes out the door.

To summarize, bargain hunters seek volatility in stock prices to find opportunities, and panicked selling creates the most volatility, usually at historically high levels. Bargain hunters seek misconception, and panicked selling is the height of misconception because of the overwhelming presence of *fear*. People's fears become exaggerated in a crisis, and so do their reactions. The typical reaction is to sell in a crisis, and the force of that selling also is exaggerated. Bargain hunters look to take advantage of temporary problems that are exaggerated in the minds of sellers because of the sellers' near-term focus. History shows that crises always appear worse at the outset and that all panics are subdued in time. When panics die down, stock prices rise.

Bargain hunters must have the right perspective to gain from these market events. Buying as the market goes into feverish selling can elevate the performance of your investment account over its lifetime. This is true no matter how experienced or inexperienced you are. If you take a long-term perspective on your investments, you will realize that an event such as the stock market crash of October 19, 1987, and the way you respond to it will be magnified over the years that follow. When you have the proper perspective, you will view these events as gifts.

Let us use as a very simple example of two investors: Mr. Steady and Ms. Wise. Both had accumulated savings of $100,000 and were looking to invest their savings in a stock brokerage account in the second week of October 1987. Both had visited their respective brokers at the beginning of the week, filled out their paperwork, and deposited their money and were ready to invest. Because they were somewhat inexperienced but cautious with their money, both had concluded independently that they would buy shares in a long-standing reputable business such as General Electric. Mr. Steady called his broker on Friday, October 16, 1987, and put in an order to buy $100,000 worth of shares in GE, but Ms. Wise decided to think more about the purchase over the weekend and give her broker a call on Monday morning. On the next Monday, October 19, 1987, both investors were shaken to discover that the stock market was experiencing the largest single-day drop in its history. It was a day that would be known forever as Black Monday, because the Dow Jones Industrial Average fell 22.6 percent in one session of trading. Mr. Steady was disturbed by the sell-off in the Dow and the instant loss of over 17 percent in his GE stock but decided it would be foolish to sell in the middle of a panic, and so he held on to his shares. Job well done, Mr. Steady.

Ms. Wise, in contrast, got a bit excited over the sell-off and decided to put in that order for GE, since surely it was trading down with the market and she would get a better bargain. She grabbed the phone and called her broker. No answer. She called again and could not reach the broker. Deciding it was important to get the stock that day, she got in her car and drove to the brokerage office to have the order placed. At the office, she walked confidently over to the broker's desk, but he was not there. Where was he? She walked behind his desk and found him hiding beneath it. She grabbed him by the ear, lifted him up, and instructed him to get on the phone and buy her that stock. He responded weakly and was as pale as a ghost but pulled it together enough to place the order. Excellent job, Ms. Wise.

Over the next 19 years, both Mr. Steady and Ms. Wise held on to their General Electric stock and watched it grow in value. Both investors decided to sell their holdings on the anniversary of Black Monday on October 19, 2006. Mr. Steady looked at the share price and used it to calculate a compounded annualized return over the last 19 years of 11.8 percent, not including dividends. Similarly, Ms. Wise was curious to know what her return had been over the last 19 years. Since that time she had studied investing and had grown into a very successful investor. She figured that because she had purchased mutual funds run by experienced bargain hunters and even dabbled in a few stocks she found to be heavily mispriced, her account's return had been an annualized 14 percent. With that in mind, she calculated her return on the GE shares—her first purchase 19 years earlier—and found that she had made an annualized 13.0 percent on the investment. Not bad at all; in fact, it was an enviable showing for her first buy in the market.

Mr. Steady with his 11.8 percent return and Ms. Wise with her 13.0 percent return both should have felt relatively good about the way they handled themselves back in 1987. However, that small 1.2 percent difference between their two returns created a large difference in the amounts of their original $100,000 investments. For instance, Mr. Steady saw his $100,000 grow to $832,519 by the time he sold his stock, but Ms. Wise, who had the good fortune of buying her shares at a better price because of the panic on Black Monday, made out far better. Ms. Wise, whose compounded return was a mere 1.2 percentage points above Mr. Steady's, saw her original $100,000 become $1,011,203.

The point is that these small differences in annualized returns, when allowed to compound over time, create very different outcomes in terms of the amount of money they create. This is the magic of compounding, and although it is not obvious to most investors, a small spread of about 3 to 4 percentage points often separates the greatest investors in the world from the rest of the pack. Taking advantage of market panics is an important method for breaking from the pack in both one's investment approach and the results that follow. If you are buying when everyone else is selling, you are not following the crowd, and your results will not follow the crowd either (they will be better). The most important thing to realize about market panics is that *all bargain hunters* should be able to capitalize on those events. Even if you have no concept of how to value a stock, you have no excuse not to add to your mutual funds. If you have the psychological ability to add to your investments during future panics, you already have distinguished yourself as a superior investor. If you can find the resolve to buy when the situation looks most bleak, you will have the upper hand in the stock market.

There is a strong historical precedent for buying in the wake of panic in the stock market, and those panics can come from a number of directions. Panicked selling can arise from a political event (threat, assassination), an economic event (oil embargo, Asian financial crisis), or an act of war (Korean War, Gulf War, September 11 attacks). Regardless of the underlying event, when the markets make a concerted effort to sell on the basis of a negative surprise, bargain hunters should be looking to buy some of the shares others wish to sell. In Uncle John's words, "Accommodate the sellers."

Table 7.1 lists a number of events that took place during the last 50-plus years that sent the stock market into a selling frenzy. In addition to listing the events and their dates, the table shows the number of days it took the market to reach a low. This gives you a rough estimate of how long it took for the selling to subside after each event. Sometimes crisis-driven selling can last for 50 days, sometimes just for 1 day. In the column labeled "Growth of $100K Precrisis" we provide an estimate of the growth of $100,000 invested in the Dow Jones Industrial Average on the day before the event and held for the following five years; in the column labeled "Growth of $100K Postcrisis," we provide the growth of $100,000 invested at the low point of the selling and held for the next five years.

Table 7.1

History of Recent Crises

Crisis	Event Date	Duration to Low (days)	% Change to Low	Growth of $100K Precrisis	Growth of $100K Postcrisis
Attack on Pearl Harbor	12/7/1941	12	−8.2%	$146,633	$166,767
Korean War	6/25/1950	13	−12.0%	$200,262	$231,698
President Eisenhower's Heart Attact	9/26/1955	12	−10.0%	$120,036	$134,239
Blue Monday—1962 Panic	5/28/1962	21	−12.4%	$149,929	$162,778
Cuban Missile Crisis	10/14/1962	8	−4.8%	$146,593	$160,313
President Kennedy Assassination	11/22/1963	1	−2.9%	$131,733	$135,918
1987 Crash	10/19/1987	1	−22.6%	$141,287	$183,380
United Airlines LBO Failure	10/13/1989	1	−6.9%	$140,451	$151,421
Persian Gulf War	8/2/1990	50	−18.4%	$162,122	$200,219
Asian Financial Crisis	10/27/1997	1	−7.2%	$107,781	$117,910
September 11	9/11/2001	5	−14.3%	$118,596	$140,039

A couple of observations can be gathered from these data. Starting with the column on the far left, we can see that a number of different events and scenarios can disrupt the stock market and create mass selling. Political events such as the outbreak of war and a threat to the nation's leadership tend to present some of the easier opportunities for a bargain hunter with a cool demeanor. Despite the psychological challenge introduced by the stock market's reaction, the most dedicated bargain hunters should be able to disregard that behavior and concentrate on the results that accrue when they are able to buy in these circumstances.

The benefits are tangible, and in each instance an investor with a long-term time horizon should gain from adding to his or her investments during these fits of selling. For evidence, see the column on the far right of Table 7.1, which shows the dollar amounts that are generated years later, when the crisis becomes a more distant memory. The circumstances of the market's sell-off may be recalled only vaguely by then, but the benefit of buying remains in clear view. Two more observations: We can see that over time there appears to be a steady stream of crisis events that lead to broad selling in the stock market. For the sake of brevity, we excluded a large number of fairly well known panics dating much farther back. For this reason, investors can be assured that there will be future instances of stock market selling that are based on a crisis or panic. However, you also may notice that these events do not happen every day. In fact, you could surmise that only a few pop up every decade.

With that said and depending on your time horizon as an investor, you need to realize that these are precious opportunities. Put another way, when these events occur in the future, you must have the perspective to pounce on them because you cannot count on their appearing every couple of years. The truth is that most sea-soned bargain hunters salivate for these events and remain in con-stant anticipation for them because of the opportunities they afford. Whenever you observe people in the stock market who want to sell, you should feel the same urgency to buy.

Despite the commonsense appeal of being a buyer when the rest of the market is selling out of fear, this is a difficult task to execute. The problem is once again that all the psychological duress that the stock market can muster will be thrown directly into your face.

Let's take the first possible consideration, which is that unless you are lucky enough to be in all cash or have a reliable crystal ball, chances are that you too will be losing money in your investments. Your inclination will be to direct your attention to protecting your-self from those losses and concentrate on solving that initial prob-lem. Obviously, if you spend this precious time worrying about your current investments, you are not taking the time to focus on what you should be doing: buying as opposed to selling. If you are selling or are focused on selling, you are following the crowd. The basic premise here is that the best time to buy is when there is blood in the streets, even if some of it is your own. Do not waste time watching your profits shrink or your losses add up. Do not go on the defensive with the rest of the market; instead, go on an offen-sive mission to find the bargains coming to the table. The goal in investing is to raise your long-term returns, not to scramble to sell. Fixate on your goal.

Although you may be facing the reality of losses in your invest-ments, you will also have to digest or cope with the deluge of neg-atively focused media attention that the event will garner. One of the simple truths in media is that negative news gets attention and positive news does not. Just as you may be daydreaming about that big sell-off, you can be sure that a news reporter somewhere is day-dreaming about the calamitous event that sparks that sell-off. You can be sure that once the bad news becomes public, a thousand Chicken Littles will come out to proclaim that the sky is falling. They will appear on the television, in the newspaper, and on the Internet and will draw a lot of attention. Smart bargain hunters keep a skeptical but open mind when processing this information. Is the sky falling? History has shown repeatedly that it is not.

A bargain hunter's role is more akin to that of Foxey Loxey, who spots the hysteria and plays it to his own advantage. Playing the role of Foxey Loxey, the fox that ate Chicken Little and her hysterical friends, is relatively difficult because the journalists covering the event are expert at focusing on the problems at hand and magnify-ing them for the public. One fear-inspiring tool that is applied often in the reporting of crisis-related selling in the stock market consists of parallels drawn between what is unfolding currently and notori-ous events from the past. Sometimes, depending on the crisis at hand, the parallels conjure up scary ghosts from market's past such as the crash of 1929, the crash of 1987, or anything related to the Great Depression. These allusions can be instructive in some cases, as we should know our history and process current events in that con-text, but these journalistic comparisons serve to direct our minds to the worst possible outcomes. For instance, during a market sell-off in 1962 known as Blue Monday, reporters for the *New York Times* referenced margin-induced selling and portrayed the similarity to events surrounding the 1929 crash. They interviewed an observer at the exchange who "was here just before the 1929 crash and wanted to see how things turned out today."

Chances are good that you have not heard of Blue Monday and even better that you have not heard of it because it was nothing like the crash of 1929. The sell-off on Blue Monday has been attributed to growing sentiment among investors and businesspeople that the Kennedy administration had an antibusiness agenda. Although the market experienced a 12.4 percent decline over the next few weeks, it was not like the crash that preceded the Great Depression, nor was there a depression. In a similar vein, on October 13, 1989, the stock market fell 6.9 percent when news broke that a planned buyout of United Airlines' parent company would not be completed because of a lack of financing. In the wake of the announcement, the stock market sold off in a panic that was based on fear that the deal's breakup signaled that more previously announced deals in the market would not receive financing. A day later, on October 14, an article in the *New York Times* was headed "Is It 1987 Again?" in reference to the 1987 crash. Put bluntly, no, it was not.

In fact, all the similarities cited by the journalist between the sell-off in 1989 and the crash in 1987 were merely *coincidences*. Finally, as you probably have guessed, when the market crashed in October 1987, the media quickly seized on the possibility that it was 1929 all over again. That event left the door open for the media to speculate on the threat of another Great Depression unfolding. The headlines read like this: STOCKS PLUNGE 508 POINTS, A DROP OF 22.6%; 604 MILLION VOLUME NEARLY DOUBLES RECORD; DOES 1987 EQUAL 1929? Fortunately for the journalist, the respondents to the interview from Wall Street quickly dispelled any notion that the crash would lead to another depression.

In spite of the ability of the media to instill fear in the market and help investors part with their stocks at lower prices, this is a blessing for the bargain hunter. The simple fact that bad news sells newspapers is good news for the bargain hunter. The public's fixation on bad news and the media's willingness to supply it to the public ensure that the stock market periodically will receive too much negative attention. Stocks will always face a threat of becoming priced too low thanks to negative attention. When we approach the situation in this light, we can think of the media as advocates of the bargain hunter that are telling stockholders to get out before it is too late. They are in a sense acting as agents on behalf of those who seek bargains: Sell your shares, run for it, the sky is falling!

Despite the ease which we can point out the merits of buying when the world is selling as well as what to expect in that environment, this task remains difficult. It is one of the few tasks in the market that require courage. It may seem funny at first, but it takes a lot of courage to step into a situation in which the majority is against you and act decisively. When there is money on the line, it is much easier to sink back into the crowd. It is always easier to go with the flow. However, in the stock market, going with the flow is an accelerated path to mediocrity.

When people are asked to describe great leaders, whether on a personal level or in the history books, the stories that often provide the best illustrations are those which illuminate a leader's behavior under great pressure. Leaders are defined by their actions when the chips are down, not when everything is going smoothly. We see this time and again in politics, sports, and business. George Washington launched successful surprise counterattacks that turned around the Revolutionary War after losing New York City. Michael

Jordan wanted the basketball in his hands when the game was on the line.

Similarly, the most successful investors are defined by their actions in a bear market, not a bull market. Making money is relatively easy when the entire stock market is rising. Aggressively seeking the opportunity provided through deep adversity when the stock market is in a free fall requires far more than the ability to analyze a company. It requires a mindset that looks for a chance to shine, and this requires confidence and courage. The only way to execute under this pressure is to have a deep-seated belief in your abilities and the conviction that you are correct in your actions.

No matter how much investors want to distinguish themselves in these tough moments, there are psychological challenges to maintaining a clear head during a sharp sell-off. One way Uncle John used to handle this was to make his buy decisions well before a sell-off occurred. During his years managing the Templeton Funds, he always kept a "wish list" of securities representing companies that he believed were well run but priced too high in the market. Taking this a step further, he often had standing orders with his brokers to purchase those wish list stocks if for some reason the market sold off enough to drag their prices down to levels at which he considered them a bargain.

For instance, if Uncle John found that a company had bright prospects or good managers but the stock price was $100 and he believed it was overpriced or near its intrinsic value, he might have an open order to purchase the shares if they fell to $60. This may seem like an extreme move, but he wanted the shares only at a price at which he felt they were a great bargain. Furthermore, for those who may balk at shares trading down 40 percent, the market has a history of doing things that seem unreasonable or unlikely. Look no farther than the 1987 crash, a 22.6 percent decline in one day. Statistically, it seems that events like this cannot occur, yet they do, and quite often. As a bargain hunter, you cannot afford to miss out on these "low-probability" events.

By keeping an open order to purchase shares at a predetermined price, you can sidestep a great deal of the pressure that comes with being a buyer when everyone else is a seller.

First and foremost, make your decision to buy when you are thinking clearly and your judgment is not being affected by the events at hand. Often in cases of market crisis selling you may be apt to second-guess your otherwise good judgment. The fact that so many people in the market are selling and pushing prices down rapidly proves that people lack sound judgment when stock market selling turns into a rout. Second, maintain your strict discipline of purchasing only stocks that you believe to be a bargain. If you operate at your own pace and carefully consider the valuation of a stock and the company it represents, you are more likely to make an accurate assessment. For instance, if a sell-off erupts in the market and you jump and buy shares of a stock you like only because they have fallen, that does not mean you have found a good bargain. Often you will find that the prices of overvalued firms fall to a level that leaves them only a little less overvalued; in that case you have not accomplished much by purchasing those shares except that they may be less expensive.

The bottom line for the strategy of placing orders well below the market price is that you are in a position to take advantage of the market's volatility. The basic idea is to harness that volatility and make it a positive force. Some of the best fits of volatility in the stock market occur when the consensus opinion is crushed by uncertainty or there has been a nasty surprise. If you do not have an eye to capitalize on these moments of duress as well as a game plan for doing so, you too will feel like you are bobbing around in the high seas on an inner tube.

One other important consideration in executing this strategy relates to the characteristics of the companies you choose. In light of the wide range of things that could spook the market into a panicked sell-off, some of which are a recession and an economic downturn, you should be careful to select companies that have a clean balance sheet. That means companies that are not encumbered by debt, and that includes companies that will not be encumbered by debt if and when times turn bad. In other words, the fact that a company does not appear to have too much debt at the moment does not mean that that amount of debt will not be too much to bear if the business environment worsens. It is important to consider the firm in both environments. If you are invested in a company that cannot handle its debt payments when sales start to fall or profit margins deteriorate, you may have made an unwise purchase.

There are two basic approaches to discovering how a company may fare if the economic environment takes a turn for the worse. The first approach is to measure just how much debt the company is carrying on its balance sheet as well as any obligations to pay others listed in the footnotes of its filings. To do this, you have to calculate some basic ratios that measure the amount of debt relative to the worth of the company as well as the amount of debt relative to the company's ability to pay the debt. There are many ratios that can be implemented in this analysis; we describe several useful ones below.

Debt-to-equity ratio = short-term debt + long-term debt ÷ shareholder's equity

This ratio is well known among analysts as a basic tool for determining whether a company owes more than it is worth. Benjamin Graham made it a basic rule to avoid companies that owe more than they are worth. Therefore, a debt-to-equity ratio greater than 1 may be a reason not to invest using his perspective.

Net-debt-to-equity ratio = (short-term debt + long-term debt) – cash ÷ shareholder's equity

This ratio is nearly identical to the one above with the exception that it assumes that debt minus the amount of cash the company has on hand is what the company really owes to its creditors.

EBITDA coverage ratio = earnings calculated before subtracting interest expense, taxes, and depreciation expense ÷ interest expense

This ratio often is used by lenders to get a quick estimate of how capable a company is of covering its interest payments. By using the calculation of earnings before subtracting interest expense, taxes, and depreciation expense, we get a thumbnail sketch of the company's earnings before it makes interest payments and tax payments or subtracts the accounting related noncash charge of depreciation. The idea is to calculate the amount of spread or cushion that the company has in its earnings before it would run into trouble with its interest payments. For example, an EBITDA coverage ratio of 6 (seen as a conservative benchmark) would mean that the company's earnings cover its interest payment six times.

Total-debt-to-trailing-12-months EBITDA ratio = short-term debt + long-term debt ÷ earnings calculated before subtracting interest expense, taxes, and depreciation expense (for the last 12 months)

Taking a similar approach to the EBITDA coverage ratio, this ratio displays how much debt the company has relative to its earnings. In this case, a ratio of 3 or below may be a conservative benchmark.

As you walk through these ratios, note that the numbers we offer as benchmarks will change with each industry. For example, a company with very stable sales and profit margins, such as a grocery store, probably can handle more debt than can a highly cyclical company that is apt to lose money briefly during a business downturn, such as a mining company.

It is important to calculate these ratios for the subject company and compare them to the same ratios calculated for other firms in the same line of business. In performing this comparison, you should obtain a quick view of which companies are taking on the most risk to their business through the use of debt. Similarly, by finding the average ratio for the industry, you can judge where your company falls in the industry in this regard.

Finally, in addition to calculating these debt ratios, it is important to examine the company's performance on the income statement over time. In doing this you will want to measure the variability of its results over time as they are subject to different business conditions in the industry or the overall economy. If the company was accustomed to losing money during any of its prior annual periods, this should be taken into consideration in purchasing its stock in case business conditions worsen. Of course, this is a worthy consideration before investing in any stock regardless of future conditions.

We have covered a lot of ground in this discussion. We have illustrated the range of crises that have occurred and discussed the benefits of investing in a crisis environment. Now let us turn our attention to a real crisis and how a real bargain hunter approached the opportunity.

On September 12, 2001 (the day after the terrorist attacks on the World Trade Center and the Pentagon), a reporter phoned Uncle John in his office in the Bahamas to get his comments and opinion on the events. Uncle John responded to the reporter as follows:

> I was in my office getting ready for another day of work, when I heard the news. I was immediately saddened from a humanitarian standpoint.
>
> From a financial standpoint, though, the attacks are of no consequence. It may whip up hundreds of millions of people into a frenzy, it certainly generates a lot of news, but it will have very, very short-lived effects.
>
> This act of terrorism isn't likely to be followed, so it will have no lasting effect on the consumer or on the world economy. In terms of any real financial impact or spiritual impact, the effects of this will be very short-lived.

Uncle John's views on the attacks reflected much of what we have observed in the large majority of the historical crises shown in Table 7.1 (page 177). What we observed and what his comments reflect is that most often in these instances of one-off political or war events, the stock market takes an initial hit and then recovers shortly afterward. Most often, these events do not affect the consumer or the economy enough to merit real concern. Regardless of historical precedent, this does not prevent market observers from fearing and exaggerating this very thing.

Despite Uncle John's view and the historical precedent set by a number of events, most observers believed that the threat to the economy from the attacks was very real, including Alan Greenspan, the chairman of the Federal Reserve, as he revealled in his book *The Age of Turbulence*. He later stated that his fears were overestimated. The fear of an economic setback resulting from the attacks was running high in the days between September 11, 2001, and the reopening of the stock market in the United States. Those concerns of a resulting recession were well publicized in the press. Below, we highlight and paraphrase excerpts from various media coverage in the days that followed the attacks.

From the *New York Times*:

A Body Blow to the Economy

The attacks that destroyed the World Trade Center towers and damaged the Pentagon brought the American economy to an unprecedented halt and made a recession far more likely than before.

From *The Wall Street Journal*:

Terrorist Attacks Raise Fears of Possible Economic Recession

WASHINGTON—Tuesday's terrorist bombings threaten to push an already fragile global economy into widespread recession, smashing consumer confidence and disrupting basic commercial functions such as air travel and financial markets.

Deadly Terror Attacks on U.S. Damage Asia's Recovery Hopes

The morning after terrorists went to war on America, the collateral damage started striking the economies of the world. Though nothing compared with the horrors on the ground in Manhattan and Washington, the day after was one the world's business people will never forget.

Deadly Terror Attacks on U.S. Hurt Europe's Recovery Hopes

The world's financial system shuddered Wednesday, as businesses and policymakers came to grips with a sobering realization: The mass terrorist strikes on America threaten to drive the global economy into recession.

From *The Economist*:

When the Economy Held Its Breath

The attack on the World Trade Centre as reduced to rubble one of the most famous symbols of American capitalism. But has it also increased the risk of a collapse in an already fragile world economy? American stockmarkets were closed this week, but the immediate answer from other markets around the globe seemed to be a tentative "Yes."

All the headlines and opening paragraphs from these articles emerged within a few days of the attacks on September 11, 2001. These articles probably were accompanied by similar ones in nearly every mass publication that went to print in the days that followed. As we can see, there was a strong consensus in the media to expect the worst in the form of a widespread *global* recession.

One problem that accompanies a shock or crisis is that although the circumstances tend to look different, by and large it remains similar to previous events, particularly when we focus on the outcome. For example, if there was one event that the September 11 attacks could have been compared to, it was the 1941 attack on Pearl Harbor. Despite this, many observers who were interviewed in the press about the similarities between the September 11, 2001, attacks and Pearl Harbor or the Cuban missile crisis commented that September 11 was much different and probably had different implications for the future. If there is one thing that bargain hunters must be prepared for, it is the seeming differences and some glaring differences between the *specific* circumstances of future crises and those of previous crises. In an article titled "Investing; Witnesses to Crises, Urging Caution" run in the *New York Times* on September 16, 2001, the journalist interviewed a number of experienced, credible, successful, and well-known veterans of Wall Street about their impressions of the September 11 attacks. The respondents described their firsthand experiences in past crises, and the excerpt below relates one gentleman's views.

> Time after time, he watched the stock market rebound from declines after shattering news. The comeback was modest after Pearl Harbor, but the Dow Jones industrial average was slightly higher a month after the attack than a day after it, Dec. 8, 1941. From a low in 1942—the bottom was when the United States won the battle of Guadalcanal—the market more than doubled, to a peak in mid-1946.
>
> Wall Street veterans interviewed after the terrorist attacks last week expressed doubts about the reliability of the historic pattern. They wondered whether the United States had indeed entered a new era, not the computer-driven economic one that some bulls had

proclaimed before the Nasdaq crash that began 18 months ago, but one in which implacable political foes create perpetual uncertainty.

This excerpt highlights one of the fixtures of investing on the heels of a crisis: Each crisis probably will look at least somewhat different from previous ones, but they generally have common elements. For instance, if we go back in imagination to the day Pearl Harbor was attacked by the Japanese, there was no real precedent for a surprise bombing. That was the first time it had happened, and so naturally observers were caught off guard. Similarly, before the Soviet Union tried to set up nuclear warheads in Cuba, had anything like that preceded it? The point is that each crisis will look different and have different circumstances, and that could confuse the interpretation of the current events in a historical context. However, if we boil these events down to their most common elements, we are likely to conclude that each was an act of war or aggression that shook people to their core. Those types of events have been going on since the beginning of time, or at least as far back as history books record. The reactions from the people involved also have been the same; shock, confusion, panic. It is all central to human nature.

In the deluge of negative forecasts that followed the attacks before the market reopened on September 17, 2001, it became clear that most, but perhaps not all, were expecting the worst. Nevertheless, it was apparent that a panicked sell-off would ensue when the U.S. market opened for trading. Always looking to take advantage of opportunity in the market, Uncle John prepared to be a buyer when all others were anxious to sell. However, the question remained: What to buy? The answer became simple when that was followed with another important question: Where is the outlook the worst? To answer that question, we look at an excerpt from an article run in the *New York Times* on September 15, 2001.

AFTER THE ATTACKS: FINANCIAL STRUGGLE

Airlines, in Search of Relief, Warn of Bankruptcy

Airline executives and analysts expressed grave concern for the industry yesterday, warning that mounting losses stemming from this week's terrorist attacks could force most of the country's major carriers into bankruptcy.

"This patient is dying very quickly," Gordon M. Bethune, the chairman and chief executive of Continental Airlines, the fifth largest carrier, said in a telephone interview, referring to the industry. "We all are going to be bankrupt before the end of the year. There is not an airline that I know of that has the excess cash to handle this."

Well, many could have guessed without this prompt that among all the stocks in the market, the airlines were standing on the shakiest ground. Airlines are notorious for running into trouble even when business conditions are relatively favorable. Similarly, many bargain hunters have dabbled in airlines only to regret it later. They arouse justifiable skepticism among investors even when the sky is sunny because of all the competitive pressures they face: rising fuel costs, bickering labor unions, regulatory issues, and so on. In September 2001 in particular, with storm clouds looming and flights grounded, the airlines were bleeding money at an estimated clip of $100 million to $275 million a day because of the heavy fixed costs accruing in the absence of revenue. To some extent the fear was justified *if* you did not believe that the government would step in and bail them out. If you believed that the government would not allow the airlines to fail, maybe you were willing to buy those stocks in the face of such extreme pessimism. Uncle John did not believe that the government would allow the airlines to fail after the attacks. With that view, he was standing directly opposite the wave of sellers who were lining up to dump their shares in airline stocks as fast as possible when the market reopened.

To execute his plan to purchase shares in the airlines, Uncle John looked at the companies and focused on the stocks that had the lowest P/E ratios. He found eight airline stocks that met his low P/E ratio criterion and placed an order with his broker to purchase any of the eight stocks that fell 50 percent in price over the course of the day when the market reopened on September 17. In our earlier discussions of the merits of purchasing stocks during a panic, we used illustrations that showed the benefits of holding for a five-year period after purchase.

We think that a long-term time horizon is well advised in most cases. In this case, however, Uncle John's intention was to capture the effects of the initial panic in those specific airline stocks but not to make them long-term holdings. Uncle John always used a method of comparison in investing, and on the basis of that analysis the airlines were comparatively the best way to capitalize on the panic. However, using the same method of comparison, he felt that from a longer-term holding perspective, at that time he would get much better performance in his Treasury strips and South Korean stocks. Those purchases were intended to be a short-term trade from the outset. He planned on holding whatever stocks he picked up in the trade for only six months.

When trading in the stock market opened on September 17, the doomsdayers were not disappointed. All the major indexes fell quickly, and the losses for the day ranged from the middle to the high single digits. The Dow Jones Industrial Average dropped 7.1 percent, the S&P 500 dropped 4.9 percent, and the NASDAQ dropped 6.8 percent. Among the airline stocks, the carnage was far greater.

Among the eight stocks that Uncle John had placed limit orders to purchase, three orders got filled. That is, three of the eight declined at least 50 percent from the open at some point during the day's trading. The three stocks that Uncle John purchased were AMR (the parent of American Airlines), Continental Airlines, and US Airways. Figures 7.1 through 7.3 illustrate the prices of the three securities beginning in September and going through the six months that followed September 17, 2001, to show Uncle John's returns over his targeted holding period.

Figure 7.1

Stock Price of American Airlines

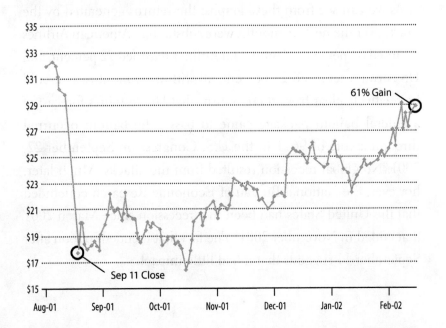

Figure 7.2

Stock Price of Continental Airlines

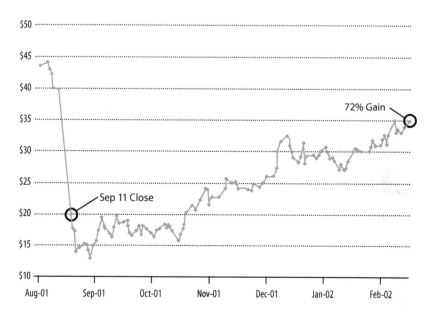

As we can see from these graphs, the returns generated by the stocks over the next six months were substantial. American Airlines returned 61 percent, Continental Airlines returned 72 percent, and US Airways returned 24 percent, all within six months. It should be relatively clear from these returns that Uncle John's forecast of a federal bailout package came to pass. The bailout occurred through a vote of 96–1 in the U.S. Congress on September 22, 2001. No global recession resulted from the attacks. Much later, however, the National Bureau of Economic Research concluded that the United States had been in a recession since March 2001 that ended in November 2001. The fact that it ended so soon after September 11 suggests that it had little impact.

Figure 7.3

Stock Price of US Airways

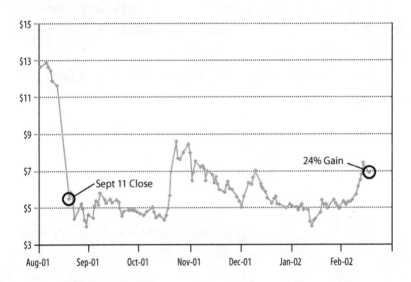

All these benign economic outcomes were portended in the numerous historical examples of how the stock market and the economy react to a crisis. However, the common precedent does not prevent investors from fearing the worst and declaring that "this time is different" from past tragedies so that the world must come to grips with a new reality. The mistakes made by people interpreting these crisis events are perhaps more forgivable than those of people who declare that this time is different at the height of a stock mania. Nevertheless, the facts speak for themselves: It pays to move opposite to the crowd, and in these instances of crisis, no matter how different the circumstances may be, the results are usually the same—you are much better off buying when the market falls out of fear. Finally, the best gift to those who look to invest during a crisis may be that each instance looks somewhat different and exact comparisons to historical crises are not easy to make. This will always serve to rattle investors. If the comparisons were easy, it is probable that there would not be a sell-off. Regardless, the wise bargain hunter is a student of history.

Bargain hunters embrace the timeless lesson from history that crisis equals opportunity.

Chapter | 8

HISTORY RHYMES

History doesn't repeat itself, but it does rhyme.
—Mark Twain

In 1997 investors worldwide were jolted by a chain reaction of financial crises referred to as the Asian financial crisis. There were several crises that affected a number of currency and stock markets around the world. The economies of the Asian countries primarily affected by the crisis were left in shambles. The situation was dire as many governments had to be rescued from mountains of debt they were unable to honor. Many banks in the affected Asian countries failed, and the local currencies lost over 50 percent of their value. In the wake of those events stock market investors saw a glass that was totally empty, but Uncle John saw a glass waiting to be refilled.

The Asian financial crisis may bring back vivid memories to some investors but only vague recollections to others, depending on age and experience. We will provide some background to describe the environment but leave technical descriptions to the academics and economists who still debate its origins. There are two schools of thought on the cause of the Asian financial crisis:

the "weak fundamentals" argument and the "financial panic" argument. The weak fundamentals theory basically states that there were macroeconomic and financial fundamental flaws in the Asian economies, and the financial panic theory blames a sudden change in investor sentiment (panicked fleeing of capital) for the bulk of the fallout. Both views have strong proponents and detractors, and we will resist exploring them in favor of focusing on the crisis in the context of the opportunity it presented to hunt for bargains.

The Asian financial crisis is acknowledged to have begun with the devaluation of Thailand's currency (the Thai baht) in July 1997. Thailand devalued its currency because it was pegged to the U.S. dollar; that means that investors can swap the two currencies at a specified rate. To accommodate currency conversions, Thailand (and any other country pegged to the U.S. dollar) had to control the growth in supply of its currency to a level proportionate to that of the United States. This essentially meant maintaining borrowing at a reasonable pace and level so that a country did not owe excessively more than its reserves of U.S. dollars.

If the two currencies are misaligned too far, lenders to the government may realize that it cannot honor its ability to convert the currencies. This realization can lead to a "run" on the currency as lenders and exponentially more investors speculating in the currency's collapse rush to sell baht and convert to U.S. dollars. If the government cannot honor those transfers, its typical response is to "devalue" the currency or release the stated pegged ratio that had been in place. An example would be if you had 10 units of the local currency that equaled 1 U.S. dollar but the government did not have enough U.S. dollars on hand to accommodate the market and responded by saying that it now takes 20 units to buy 1 U.S. dollar.

The local currency buys far fewer U.S. dollars, or it takes a lot more local currency to buy a dollar. Either way you look at it, it is a bad deal for people who want the government to honor its prior policy of converting local currency to U.S. dollars. If the market senses that there is a high probability that the government will not be able to honor its obligation to convert the currency, a mad dash may ensue to pull money out before the government changes the peg. The end result is a panicked selling of the government's currency that drives its price down as well as the prices of assets denominated in that currency, such as stocks.

This dynamic became catastrophic for banks in a country such as Thailand, which secured its capital for lending by borrowing at the low interest rates for the U.S. dollar. The bottom line is that if the local currency drops in value, loans taken out in U.S. dollars effectively increase in size. If U.S. dollar loans increase too much, it can bankrupt the bank. Thus, when the Thai government formally acknowledged that its finances were out of order and removed the peg on its currency, that selling activity created huge losses not only for the Thai baht's value but also for everything denominated in baht. Shortly after that event, investors cast a skeptical eye on a number of other Asian countries whose currencies were pegged to the U.S. dollar that had been experiencing a boom in investment and heavy borrowing. The newly heightened awareness that resulted from Thailand's actions caused stronger scrutiny of the remaining "Asian miracles" and precipitated heavy selling in those countries' currencies. You may wonder how a government's finances could get so poor in the first place, but it is actually not that unusual.

However, part of the problem in the case of Asia was that a group of countries referred to as the Asian miracles had posted strong growth rates in their economies over a number of years, and that attracted investors. Over time the heavy investment led to too much money coming into the country, followed by overdevelopment in some sectors of the economy. The overdevelopment would not generate the returns necessary to pay back lenders or investors. In some ways, those countries were victims of their own success. Nevertheless, the end result was a chain reaction of selling in those countries' currencies as investors rushed to pull their money out as fast as possible. The chain reaction leaped from Thailand to Malaysia, Indonesia, the Philippines, Singapore, and finally South Korea. Eventually, similar fundamental dynamics led to deeply depressed currency values in Russia, Brazil, and Argentina in the years that followed.

Among all the bombed-out countries left in the wake of the crisis, South Korea was the one that caught Uncle John's attention as a bargain hunter. Truth be told, he had been attracted to the economic fundamentals of that country for a few decades. In a book about Uncle John published in 1983 called *The Templeton Touch*, there was an interview and discussion about his prescient investments in Japan during the 1960s. Over the course of the discussion the question naturally arose as to what Uncle John thought might be "the next Japan" from an investment standpoint. His answer was South Korea. However, much like his original objection to placing his clients in Japanese investments, South Korea had a policy of capital controls that restricted foreign investors from removing their funds, and that prevented him from investing Templeton Funds money in South Korea. Regardless of the environment at that time, he believed that South Korea, like Japan before it, eventually would relax the laws that restricted the removal of foreign capital.

The reasons Uncle John may have considered South Korea to be the next Japan for investors could be seen in their striking similarities from an economic standpoint. South Korea in effect was implementing the same game plan that had propelled Japan to economic success after its devastation in World War II. South Korea had the same basic circumstances when it emerged from the Korean War. It was a country that was left in an economic quagmire and forced to rebuild. Although it took a bit longer to get on the right track, South Korea often is referred to as the *best* case of an economy rising from poverty to industrial power.

Let us review the basic actions that South Korea and Japan took to elevate their economic profiles. First, both countries had heavy rates of domestic saving that funded investment in their economies. Second, both were exporters but also, and perhaps more important, *ambitious* exporters. In other words, Japan was dismissed as an unsophisticated producer of trinkets and cheap goods when it began rebuilding its economy after World War II. South Korea had that reputation as it embarked on its economic journey to emerge as a powerful industrial nation. It has been noted that well before South Korea developed its heavy industrial capabilities, it was known for exporting textile goods, and in its early stages of development its top exports were all basic "cheap" items. For instance, in 1963 South Korea's third biggest export was human hair wigs. South Korea was directing itself down a path of progressive industrialization, and its economy was one of the fastest growing in the world as measured by growth in GDP. The country's economy had the highest average growth in the world over the 27-year period leading up to the Asian financial crisis.

Over the same period, the government's direction of resources and capital into export-led businesses transformed the export mix from textiles and wigs to electronics and automobiles. In addition to the overall higher growth rate, South Korea was able to resist significant pauses in its growth as only the oil shock crisis of 1980 derailed a long period of uninterrupted high growth (see Figures 8.1 and 8.2).

One of the features that accompanied South Korea's transition toward a more sophisticated economy was a lessening dependence on foreign borrowing and an increasing level of domestic saving that occurred during the 1980s. Much like Japan as it reemerged from World War II, South Korea built its economic power on the back of high savings rates rather than large borrowings. Although both countries began their growth under a program of foreign aid (Japan after World War II and Korea after the Korean War), those regimes quickly created a backdrop of financial independence for their capital needs (see Figures 8.3 and 8.4).

Much like Japan before it, South Korea had a savings rate well in excess of the worldwide norm. In fact, South Korea's savings rate was above 30 percent until the 2000s.

Despite all these positives and striking similarities between South Korea and Japan, Uncle John never invested there over that period because South Korea had notoriously stringent capital controls as well as restricted access to its financial markets. For instance, it was only in 1992 that foreign investors were allowed to put any money into South Korea. Until at least 1992 restrictions on all types of money transactions, regardless of citizenship, were onerous.

Figure 8.1

South Korea Annual Growth Rate in GDP, 1971–1997

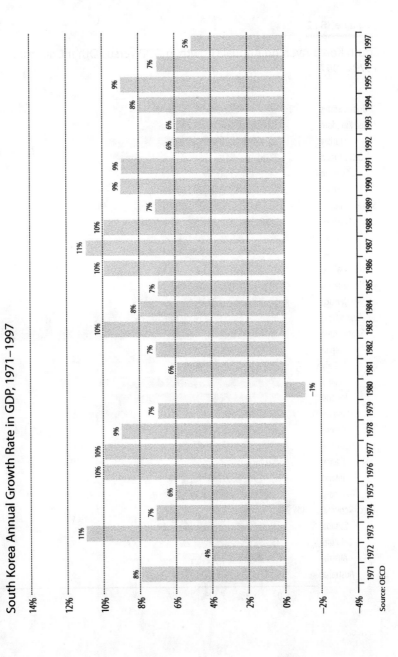

Source: OECD

Figure 8.2

South Korea Average Annual Growth in GDP versus Other Countries,
1970–1997

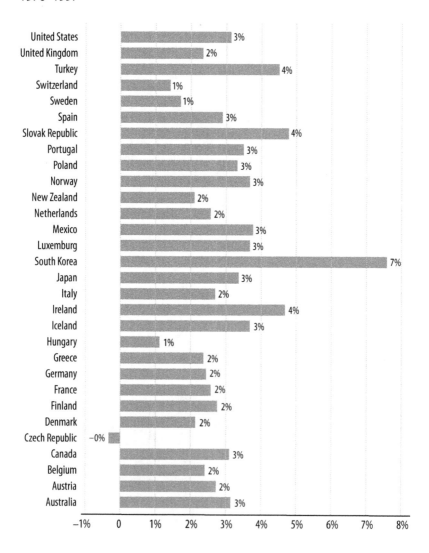

Source: OECD

Figure 8.3

South Korea Annual Gross National Savings Rate, 1980–1997

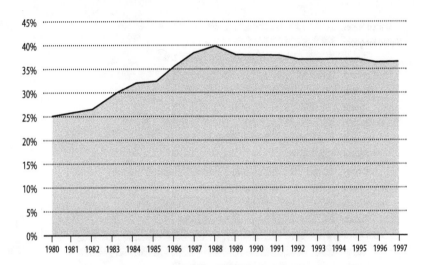

South Koreans were not free to borrow money from abroad, they were not free to take dollars out of the country, and any company or person bringing foreign currency into the country had to convert it immediately to Korean won. Those restrictions had some residual effects on the South Korean economy that became hindrances when the stock market was opened to foreign investors. One effect was that the previous scarcity of foreign exchange kept it in high demand among businesses, and the large industrial conglomerate exporters (conglomerates in South Korea often are referred to as *chaebols*) favored by the government were the beneficiaries. The chaebols had better access to reserves to transact business. The allocation of resources such as reserves to the chaebols made them very powerful.

Figure 8.4

Average Gross National Savings Rates by Country, 1987–1997

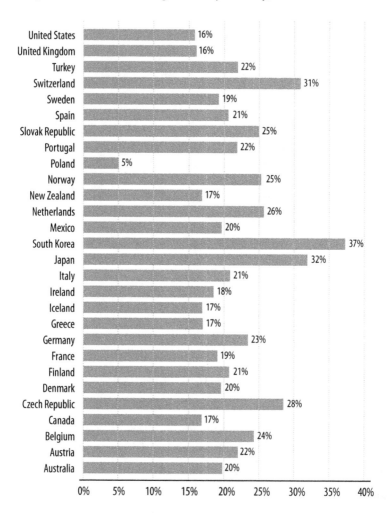

The chaebols used their access to funds to grow and take on debt at will. The government's favoritism toward them meant that the chaebols could invest and grow without the natural resistance of profit-driven lenders that eventually cut off companies that take on too much debt. The huge debt burdens of the chaebols fueled a large part of the negative perception that led to the crisis. When instances of cronyism and corruption were uncovered years later, it fueled a perception that all the large exporters were corrupt. That exaggerated perception caused some foreign investors to stay away and helped lower the general prices that investors were willing to pay for Korean stocks.

Despite its strong economic performance derived from following the example of Japan, South Korea in late 1997, after the eruption of the Asian financial crisis, found itself in a strange position of weakness. The country agreed to open its markets to unprecedented levels as a condition of receiving outside financial aid. South Korea, which had been hailed for demonstrating the fastest rise from a war-torn nation to an industrial powerhouse, appeared to be flat on its back in late 1997. The country was caught up in the crisis because of excessive leverage in most of its prized chaebols, which collectively were burdened with debt.

When some of the noted chaebols, such as Kia Motors, Jinro, and Haitai, sought bankruptcy protection for failure to cover their interest payments in the summer of 1997, investors turned an increasingly critical eye toward South Korea and its financial situation. The fear was that those bankruptcies and ones that could follow would feed back into the banking system. Similarly, with large proportions of debt denominated in foreign currency, the appearance of risk was high. From a perception standpoint, outside observers had no way to measure the potential severity of the problem, because disclosure was limited and the banks were controlled by the government. Without being able to measure the problem, investors assumed the worst.

However, overall South Korea's government borrowing was relatively modest at less than 20 percent of GDP before the crisis.

Nonetheless, South Korea had a real problem: A much larger percentage of its loans were in short-term maturities that had to be rolled over or extended on a regular basis. That meant that the country's debt had to be renewed in the middle of a regional financial meltdown. The problem of defaulting borrowers in the Korean chaebol system was made worse by the simultaneous financial difficulties in Thailand and Malaysia.

One problem Korea shared with those countries was that they all seemed to have one major lender in common: Japan. When the Japanese realized that they had so much exposure to the spreading defaults and bankruptcies in the region, they did not hesitate to pull the plug on South Korea. The result was a near cessation of lending activity to South Korea despite the fact that its situation was not as dire as that of other countries. Nevertheless, currency speculators relentlessly sold short the Korean won on the basis of the deteriorating financial conditions. At the same time, South Korea tried to support its currency's value in the market by purchasing it with its precious stash of foreign reserves. That was futile; as the country wasted its reserves by purchasing the won to keep its price up on the open market, it became clear that South Korea was headed for trouble. When South Korea no longer could afford to defend its currency in the open market, the won collapsed in value at the end of 1997 and took down all the asset markets with it, including the stock market.

It was during those last months of 1997 that South Korea was forced to resort to "the lender of last resort" for troubled economies, the International Monetary Fund (IMF). The IMF is an economic coalition in which countries pay into a "fund" over time with the understanding that if they run into a financial crisis, those payments will be extended to them as a loan to resolve the crisis. Typically, the IMF will impose conditions on a country to receive the loan, such as policy changes in its economy. This certainly was going to be the case with South Korea in late November 1997 as it went to the IMF to resolve its liquidity crisis.

South Korea received a proposal for a $58.5 billion loan package from the IMF to see it through the crisis, but the package came with heavy conditions. The primary demands were for South Korea to open its financial markets to foreign investors and remove inefficient firms from the market. Although initially reluctant to agree to the reforms, South Korea began to implement the changes in early 1998. The two reforms shook the national mindset. The country was proud of its prior economic success and saw the crisis as only a temporary setback. People with that belief system chafed under the idea that it should be told to shut down inefficient businesses. South Koreans were accustomed to holding a job indefinitely regardless of performance because of labor restrictions.

The idea of firms shutting down and employees being laid off was unusual. Similarly, the country had been subject to colonization during its political history and was deeply wary of foreign ownership of or involvement in its businesses. Therefore, the notion of opening its markets to more foreign ownership was tough to swallow. Before long, local workers began to refer to the IMF as the "I Am Fired." Despite the seemingly drastic changes and any near-term pain that would follow, those moves were, as designed, very friendly to investors outside Korea. However, one big problem remained: The economy was flat on its back, and there were divisive elements that desired a return to "the old ways" of protectionism and heavy capital controls. In the middle of its IMF aid package, South Korea raised its interest rates substantially to prevent further deterioration in its currency (making it more attractive to own or more expensive to borrow and sell short). As the country raised interest rates, the growth of the domestic economy growth was choked off and a recession became inevitable. Because of those variables of policy adoption and recession, investors were highly skeptical about the country's prospects—except, perhaps, for one. In January 1998 Uncle John was ready to bargain-hunt in Korea, and the *Wall Street Journal* picked up on his move:

John Templeton Makes Bet on Battered Korea Market
By KAREN DAMATO
January 2, 1998

The battered South Korean stock market has lured big-name bargain-hunter Sir John Templeton. The Bahamas-based investor says he has pumped money into a number of Korean-stock vehicles over the past month. Among them: Matthews Korea Fund, a San Francisco-based mutual fund whose 64% decline through Tuesday ranks it as one of 1997's worst-performing U.S.-based funds.

"I think the Korean market is somewhere near the bottom," the 85-year-old Sir John said in a phone interview Wednesday. "All my investment career, I have always tried to buy at the point of maximum pessimism. . . . The pessimism in Korea has been so intense in recent months."

Sir John, a global-investment pioneer who founded the Templeton fund group and later sold it to Franklin Resources, declined to say how much he has invested in Korea. He said the sum is "very small" in relation to his total portfolio. But his recent investment in the Matthews Korea Fund, which appears to be at least several million dollars, is certainly a big deal to that small fund, which describes itself as the only open-end U.S. mutual fund that specializes in Korea.

In spite of the looming certainty of a serious recession in South Korea and the latent possibility that the government would rescind its newfound market openness in favor of protectionist measures, Uncle John saw a stock market that was thoroughly depressed and, in his formulation, reaching the point of maximum pessimism. In terms of politics, he believed that South Korea would continue to accept the idea of mobile capital flows rather than clamping down on the flow of money into and out of the country.

Thus, just as all the investors in the market were storming the exits and turning their backs on South Korea, there were two very positive signals for the bargain hunter. First, as long as you believed that Korea would play fair and not return to its Draconian capital controls, the market was about to become much friendlier to outside investors. Second, stock prices had fallen dramatically relative to earnings in the span of a couple of months and had the lowest P/E ratios in the market. If you believed that over the next couple of years the county would rebound to its old healthy growth and prosperity, those stocks were excellent bargains. Putting it all together, if you could look past the near-term disarray, the country had an attractive long-term future and the stocks were dirt cheap. It was the perfect recipe for a bargain hunter with enough courage to step into the void. As Figure 8.5 shows, the representative P/E ratio in the South Korean market had fallen from 20× earnings per share (EPS) to a level below 10× EPS. This collapse in the P/E ratio represented a fire sale because of the near-term poor outlook for South Korea.

Figure 8.5

South Korean Stocks Price/Earnings Ratio, 1997

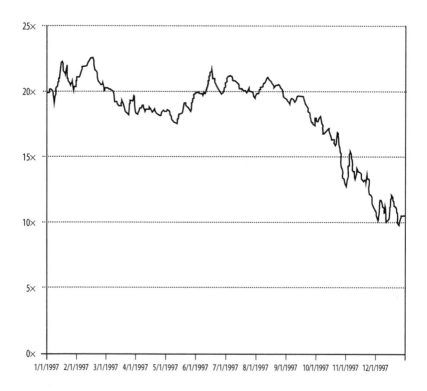

As you probably noticed in the report from *The Wall Street Journal*, Uncle John chose a mutual fund as one of his key vehicles for investing in the depressed Korean market. This strategy is instructive for bargain hunters from all walks and backgrounds. Uncle John was as comfortable as anyone on the planet picking a stock to buy in Korea, and he did buy some individual stocks in that country. However, for a true bargain hunter, it is unnecessary to dig in and buy individual stocks in every circumstance, particularly if you are making an investment at a point of maximum pessimism when everyone is avoiding a particular market for stocks. The underlying reality is that most often a differentiating factor between an average investor and a great investor is a willingness to buy what others do not rather than being a genius stock picker. If you can train yourself to think in this manner and fight the innate tendency to avoid bad-looking situations without further scrutiny, you have won a major battle that most investors, no matter how intelligent, consistently lose.

The fact that you have outsourced your stock picking to someone else, such as a mutual fund, does not mean that you are completely off the hook. It is important that you investigate these hired bargain hunters and their methods. One way to approach researching mutual funds is to look for a fund manager who basically is acting as an agent on your behalf. This seems obvious, but if you have formulated beliefs on investing, your goal should be to locate fund managers who are like-minded. You are a general, and these are your lieutenants in the field. For instance, when Uncle John made an investment in the Matthews Korea Fund on the heels of the financial crisis, he was placing his money in the hands of someone who thinks and operates much along the same lines as he does. This is the basis for mutual fund investing, or it should be. However, most mutual fund investors are prone to examining recent returns and investing in the funds with the best recent performance.

What may be lost on investors when they allocate capital this way is the fact that they could be investing at the top of a trend in the market or in a basket of story stocks that are popular. Chasing good performance in mutual funds is often no different from chasing good performance in individual stocks. It would be a ridiculous practice as a bargain hunter to buy stocks only on the basis of what has been going up in price. Investing in mutual funds solely because they have gone up in value is equally hazardous. At the same time, it would be reckless to exclude investment funds because they have had a good performance. The idea, after all, is to make money from your investments. The only way to make a sound decision is to investigate the methods and processes employed by fund managers. In our case, we are in search of managers who apply a bargain-hunting approach, focus on long-term projections in valuing a company, and are eager to take advantage of downward swings in the market.

In the case of the Matthews Korea Fund in late 1997, Uncle John was able to collate all his personal ideas into one investment vehicle. First, Uncle John was particularly keen on investing in South Korea. Nearly all other investors had rushed out of the market and pushed stock prices down to exceedingly low levels compared with earnings and the future growth potential of earnings. Second, at the time, the Matthews Korea Fund was the only mutual fund in the United States that focused wholly on the Korean market. Third, upon interviewing the fund's manager, Paul Matthews, Uncle John found an investor who had studied his career for many years and patterned many of the Matthews Fund's investment methods after his. A review of the fund's prospectus would reveal that Paul Matthews and his associates have many of the same philosophies on stock selection and the Asian markets as Uncle John. For instance, whereas many investors tend to focus on the past or current shortfalls in the practices of the governments in Asia, both Matthews and Uncle John believe that many of the markets will continue to open. This was the basic philosophy that Uncle John followed when he first invested in Japan, and in early

1998 he had the same belief in South Korea. Perhaps not surprisingly, the Matthews Fund managers believed the same thing.

The important thing to focus on is finding a mutual fund manager who primarily acts as an extension of your approach. In other words, you have established an investment philosophy and now are looking to outsource the nitty-gritty of stock selection. If you focus solely on the recent performance of funds, you are joining a crowd of mutual fund investors who tend to buy funds too late and sell them too early. If this pattern of investing sounds analogous to buying popular stocks too late and selling unpopular stocks too soon, you are ready to bargain-hunt for mutual funds. The truth is that bargain hunters should look to buy mutual funds after their performance has been bad rather than good, provided that the managers are capable investors.

Any investors who had focused solely on the results of the Matthews Korea Fund would have avoided it in early 1998. Managing a fund invested in Korea led to unavoidable losses during 1997 as the Asian financial crisis found its way over to this country. In fact, Matthews was cited as one of the worst-performing funds in the United States in 1997. Despite that poor performance, there was nothing wrong with the fund managers; the relentless selling of Korean shares by others accounted for the decline in performance (see Figure 8.6).

In this case, we are observing the performance of a good manager in a bad market. Understanding this relationship and spotting future ones are critical because this becomes an enabling component to your investment strategy. Put more plainly, it enables you to buy into a fund, just as you would an individual stock, when the situation looks the worst. Obtaining this enabling mindset for

Figure 8.6

Matthews Korea Fund Daily Net Asset Values, 1997

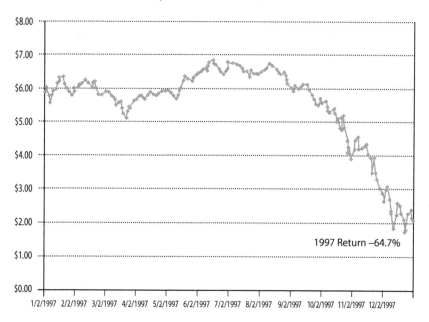

1997 Return −64.7%

mutual fund investing is identical to doing the same thing in stock purchasing. Both require study, research, and effort, to say the least. However, once you have gained comfort from your research, you should have the conviction to buy when others are selling, whether it's a mutual fund or an individual stock.

The most important considerations in investigating a mutual fund center on its approach to investing, which should mirror yours. If your idea is to buy assets for less than they are worth, you need to make sure that the managers handling your money are doing the same thing. How do they calculate the fair value of a stock? *Do* they calculate the fair value of a stock? How do they determine that a stock has value? If you think it is futile or meaningless to base an investment decision on the next quarter's earnings report of a company, you need to make sure your fund managers feel the same way. Investigate their holding periods. If you think investors should buy a stock as cheaply as possible and patiently wait for returns over the next several years, you need to see how long the manager holds the average stock in his or her portfolio. If a manager claims to purchase stocks with low P/E ratios, take the mutual fund's list of holdings and calculate the average P/E of the fund.

There are a number of ways to discover the true philosophies of a manager, starting with asking some commonsense questions and doing your homework. A number of third-party services spend all their time researching mutual funds and their managers. Using these resources frees you to study their analyses and follow up with your own questions to the manager. A provider called Morningstar is a good place to start.

When Uncle John made his investment in the Matthews Korea Fund in late 1997, he put himself in the right place at the right time. Although it took another 10 or 11 months for South Korea to dust itself off from the crisis in late 1997, the stock market eventually rallied. Figure 8.7 tells the tale of how Uncle John's original investment in the fund increased 267 percent in just two years. The fund enjoyed an unusual but uplifting distinction of going from being one of the funds with the *worst performance in 1997* to becoming the fund with the *absolute best performance in the market in 1999.*

That performance did not go unnoticed as the fund was profiled in *The Wall Street Journal* in July 1999 for posting the best one-year performance. As you read the following article, bear in mind the time period and how unlikely it was for a value manager to take the top honor; this is the backbone argument for global investing.

Figure 8.7

Matthews Korea Fund Daily Net Asset Values, 1998–1999

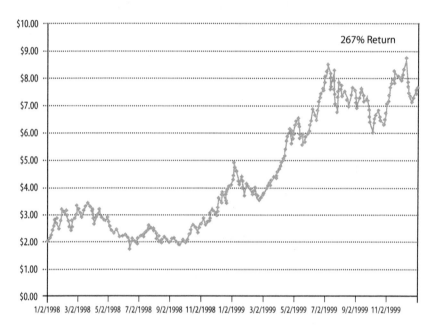

Here's to the Winners: An Asia, a Value and a Growth Fund
By DANIELLE SESSA
July 6, 1999

Matthews Korea Fund knocked last quarter's one-year winner, Internet Fund, off the pedestal with a colossal 278.5% return by focusing on that Asian nation.

One-Year Winner

Looking for a fund with sizzling triple-digit returns? Forget all those flashy Internet funds and set your sights on South Korea. Matthews

Korea Fund, managed by Paul Matthews, scored its huge return over one year by investing in that nation.

But things weren't always so rosy for the fund, part of Matthews International's lineup of five Asian-stock funds. Just after the Korea fund was launched in early 1995, the country's economy took a wrong turn. Then, two years later, the entire Asian region was rocked by a broad economic slowdown.

Matthews Korea posted negative returns for its first three years, including a gut-wrenching 65% decline in 1997. "Obviously, we had not anticipated the extent of the decline in the financial markets in the period immediately after launching the funds," says Mr. Matthews, who runs his firm from San Francisco and lived in Hong Kong in the 1980s.

The fund made headlines in late 1997, when big-time investor Sir John Templeton decided to plunge into the depressed Korean market by putting some of his money into Matthews Korea. A spokesman for the fund said that to the best of his knowledge, Sir John is still invested in the fund.

Whereas most value investors in the United States were befuddled by the Internet frenzy, Uncle John was ringing up the best returns the market could offer. This is the virtue of global bargain hunting. Being a devout bargain hunter in only the United States would have kept you on the sidelines in 1999. In contrast, being a global bargain hunter would have produced even better performance than was available gambling in the greatest stock mania of modern times. Bargain hunting trumps the greater fool theorem once again.

Although the initial success of investing in South Korea after the Asian financial crisis was stunning, Uncle John was still spotting bargains in that country many years later. A good example occurred in August 2004, when Uncle John became interested in the stock of the Korean car manufacturer Kia Motors. Kia represents another example of Uncle John's time-tested method of comparison shopping for bargains. There were a number of attributes of the stock and the company that piqued Uncle John's interest. Kia's P/E ratio was exceedingly low, and when he compared it with the company's long-term growth rate in earnings per share, it appeared to be a good bargain. Kia carried a P/E ratio of 4.8× EPS in late August 2004. That compared favorably with the P/E ratio of General Motors in the United States, which at the time was 5.9× EPS. Kia's long-term growth rate in EPS made it even more compelling compared with GM, as its EPS was growing at almost 28 percent a year. In contrast, GM's growth rate in EPS had been in a steady decline over the last five years. Uncle John was impressed with Kia as a company. He believed that the manufacturer had created tremendous value for its customers by selling a nice car at a low price while maintaining a net profit margin three times as large as that of GM. He found the stock to be such a bargain that he put $50 million of his money into the security.

The results were impressive as the stock increased 174 percent by the end of December 2005. What perhaps is even more interesting is that not long after the stock had more than doubled in 2005, Uncle John decided that it was time for a new car. The salt and weather conditions in the Bahamas can be very tough on automobiles, and his old Lincoln Town Car needed replacement. Uncle John had been impressed with the value in Kia cars, and so he thought he should look at buying one to replace his old car. He went to a Kia dealership and was just as impressed with the cars in person but left the dealership without purchasing a car. When he returned to the office, his longtime assistant, Mary Walker, asked him why he had not bought the car. His simple reply was "Too expensive for me." Later, Mary finally persuaded Uncle John to go back and get the car, saying, "I knew he wanted to buy it, but the man just doesn't spend money." Always true to form, Uncle John never let his immense success change his thrifty behavior. Once a bargain hunter, always a bargain hunter.

If some elements of this incident seem similar to the circumstances surrounding Uncle John's investment in Japan some 40 years earlier, that is not a coincidence. The two countries resembled each other in the structure of their economies and their paths to industrial power. Both applied the same strategies to achieve industrial power: heavy saving, early capital controls, and an untiring drive to become an exporter of sophisticated industrial goods. The majority of investors turned their backs on the two stock markets during a period of temporary weakness, only to return when the long-term strength of the economies again became evident.

Bargain hunters who understand history, focus on the long term, and seek to buy at the point of maximum pessimism can appreciate the fact that these patterns repeat themselves over time, again and again. Different place, different time; same story, same results. While you may not be able to identify the *exact* repeating circumstances of emerging industrial powers in the future experiencing temporary problems you can be sure to find some that rhyme.

Chapter | 9

WHEN BONDS ARE NOT BORING

An investment in knowledge always pays the best interest.
—Benjamin Franklin

In early March 2000, just a week or two before the peak and subsequent collapse in the NASDAQ that signified the end of the dot-com mania, Uncle John gave an interview to a publication called *Equities* magazine in which the editor and Uncle John discussed at length the riskiness of the Internet bubble. Uncle John went on to discuss the Internet bubble in the context of prior manias, including U.S. railroads in the nineteenth century and twentieth-century bubbles in electronics, automobiles, airplanes, radios, and televisions. He concluded by saying that the current Internet bubble was by far the biggest of them all. He figured that the mania closest to it that he could identify was the stock market bubble during the 1980s in Japan, but that was still smaller and took 20 years to develop.

Inevitably, the conversation turned to obtaining Uncle John's investment advice for the publication's readers in the face of growing risk in the stock market. We know from Chapter 6 on the Internet bubble that as the interview was being conducted, Uncle John had built a heavy inventory of short positions in technology stocks that were on the verge of generating substantial returns. However, that would have been risky advice to the readers of a magazine, and Uncle John has always been extraordinarily careful in handling others' money directly or through investment advice. To get Uncle John's advice, we pick up the conversation from the interview:

> EQUITIES: As the editor of a magazine named EQUITIES, I don't know what to advise my readers to do.
>
> Templeton: That's not too hard. Tell your readers to buy bonds. There is a tradition throughout human history that bonds have been the normal way for a long term investor to invest. It's just been that for a very large part of the twentieth century when stock markets were unreasonably low they were better buys than bonds. But right now bonds are the best buy.

For anyone reading that interview in hopes of finding a novel stock pick, it must have been disappointing to hear the word *bonds*. Most investors hear that word and immediately get an overwhelming sense of sleepiness. Perhaps it elicits a yawn, or maybe their eyes glaze over and they fall into a boredom-induced coma. Bonds are dull and unexciting. Bonds are for the elderly to draw steady income when they retire. Bonds were a *phenomenal* investment strategy in March 2000.

As much as we hope to avoid boring our readers, some minor background on bonds will help explain the strategy that Uncle John implemented in the bond market.

A bond is a security that entitles its holder to be repaid an amount owed by another entity. The borrower that makes the bond payments can be a company, a government, a government agency, or a pool of borrowers such as homeowners making mortgage payments or even borrowers repaying credit card bills. The point is that almost any type of borrowing can be turned into a bond that trades in the bond market.

In their most conventional form, bonds are issued at a face value, for example $1,000. This means that as an investor, you pay $1,000 for a bond when it is issued; the borrower gets the use of your $1,000 and the money from all the other bonds that it sold in the market at that time. In exchange, the borrower has agreed to repay you, the investor, the money you lent plus a charge for interest. Let's say that your bond charges the borrower 7 percent interest. In that case, you will receive annual interest coupons of 7 percent during the life of the bond: $70 a year for each $1,000 bond. Often the borrower makes semiannual payments, and in that case you would receive two payments a year, one every six months, of $35. If you hold the bond over its entire life, once the bond reaches maturity you will have collected the interest payments and in addition will be repaid your original $1,000.

This is the basic idea of a bond. The borrower gets the money and repays it over time, depending on the way the bond is structured. Bonds, just like stocks, trade in an open market and can change hands in the market the way stocks do. In other words, bond investors do not necessarily hold their bonds until maturity and collect the payments. Bond investors can operate the way stock bargain hunters do and look for mispricings, good deals, and so on.

This leads us to the next brief overview, which explains what determines the price of a bond.

If you remember only one thing about bonds, it should be this: Bond prices and interest rates move in opposite directions. If interest rates go up, bond prices go down. If interest rates go down, bond prices go up. To get an insight into why this relationship exists, it helps to know what makes up an interest rate.

An interest rate is stated as one number, for example, 5 percent, but it actually represents the sum of three different numbers. To begin, there is what is known as a risk-free rate. This is the first number to consider. The term *risk-free rate* refers to the interest that is charged to a borrower who has virtually no risk of default. The only borrowers who can claim that they never default are governments. Therefore, the risk-free rate is usually synonymous with the interest rate that a government such as the U.S. government offers on its bonds. We use the term only for the sake of nomenclature, because as we have seen from the last chapter as well as numerous other examples not discussed in this book that governments have been known to default on their obligations. Nevertheless, investors have come to recognize U.S. Treasuries as having no risk of default, and that is not off base. In summary, the interest charged on a U.S. Treasury bond such as a 5- or 10-year bond often is cited as the risk-free rate because it is accepted widely that a government such as the U.S. government will not default (it can always print more money).

The second number that is part of an interest rate is called *expected inflation*. This number is built into the interest rate charged because one of the large risks that bondholders face is an increase in inflation. This makes good sense because if you are receiving a fixed interest rate over a period of 5 to 30 years, it is easy to see that a large rise in inflation could erode the purchasing power of a dollar. Think about it this way: If you are receiving a fixed payment of, say, $500 a year every year for the next 30 years and there is a large rise in inflation, the value of your $500 will decrease over time as a result of the effects of rising prices and money's lower purchasing power compared with rising prices. Therefore, receivers of fixed interest payments try to protect themselves by including a projection of inflation in an interest rate.

The third number that is included in an interest rate takes into account the creditworthiness of a borrower. Bondholders want to be compensated for their risk, or the probability that they will not be repaid. With this in mind, the interest rate charged to a company with a shaky financial history will include a larger factor for the risk of default than will the rate for a borrower such as the U.S. Treasury, where the risk of default is zero. This *credit spread* becomes a basis for judging the riskiness of a bond issue, at least from the perspective of the market. For example, if the five-year U.S. Treasury bond yields 5 percent but our company issues five-year bonds that must be priced at 8 percent to find buyers, the difference of 3 percent becomes a proxy for the added risk of default on the bonds. If a company similar to ours must issue bonds at 9 percent, it is assumed to carry an even higher risk.

Let's take this information and put it to work. Since we know that the first rule in bonds is that a bond price moves in the opposite direction from the movement in interest rates, what do you suppose will happen if we are bondholders and economists project a rise in inflation from 2 percent a year to 3 percent a year? Well, this will increase interest rates, and (holding the other two components the same) the price of our bond will fall. Similarly, if we are holding the bonds of a company that has hit a rough patch and analysts believe that the company may not be able to repay its bondholders, the credit spread, or risk of default, will rise and the price of our bond will fall. Finally, if the Federal Reserve Bank of the United States takes measures to raise interest rates, the risk-free rate will rise and cause our bond price to fall. As you can see, there are three basic drivers to an interest rate. Taking it a step further, those drivers mean that there are three basic drivers to the price of a bond in the market.

Now that we have the basics covered, we need to introduce one more issue. When Uncle John bought bonds to execute his investment strategy, he bought a special type of Treasury bond that requires some explanation. Instead of buying a bond that comes with regular, predictable interest payments, he bought a bond with *zero coupon* payments. In other words, rather than receiving the periodic payments as a separate distribution, the bond is issued at less than its face value and the price of the bond increases over time to reflect the expected accumulation of interest. These types of bonds have become prevalent over the last few decades, and when they are government bonds, they often are referred to as Treasury strips. The name *strip* comes from the original practice of "stripping" the coupon payments of interest from the bond and separating the bond into its two components: the repayment of the principal and the payment of interest. The idea behind a zero coupon bond or principal-only strip is that you buy the bond at a deep discount to its face value, which is, let's say, $1,000, and over the life of the bond its price will increase until it matures and is worth $1,000.

Thus, in the case of a 30-year zero coupon bond that pays 5 percent annual interest on a semiannual basis, the investor will pay about $227 and collect $1,000 on the date the bond matures. The difference between the $227 and $1,000 that accumulates is known as *imputed interest,* or the amount of interest that will be collected over the life of the bond. If the bondholder holds the zero coupon bond over its entire 30-year period until receiving his or her $1,000, the bondholder essentially will be guaranteed an annual return of 5 percent.

If the interest rate environment changes, the price of the bond will change in the open market, and an investor may take advantage of the change in the bond price. One way to think about this is that if you buy a bond on the basis of a 5 percent return, you are guaranteed that return if you hold the bond until you are repaid your $1,000, but if interest rates go down while you are holding the bond and the bond price rises, you can take advantage of the price rise and sell the bond in the market. Thus, your zero coupon bond features more volatility in the open market and gives you the ability to capture "capital gains" exactly the way a stockholder who owns a stock that has gone up in price does. The capital gains could be generated by a changing interest rate environment in which rates are declining and bond prices are rising.

Let's return to Uncle John's advice to purchase bonds in March 2000. There were two solid reasons to make that recommendation. The first is based on the time-tested method of comparison when one is bargain hunting. Uncle John's basic rule states that you should sell a holding when you have found something with 50 percent better value. If you were an investor in the United States in early 2000 and were not investing in some of the very few bargain stock markets available, such as South Korea, your options were limited. Uncle John believed that most of the stock markets, including many around the world, were priced too high in relation to earnings, growth, and most other measures used to value stocks.

Therefore, from a commonsense perspective, it was a relatively bad idea to purchase stocks that easily could return to more normal P/E levels, which were lower than where they were in March 2000. In other words, it appeared that many stock markets ultimately would fall in price and lose value. In early 2000 Uncle John believed that at some time over the next three years the NASDAQ would fall 50 percent from its high. Using this estimation of potential losses in the NASDAQ and the view that this decline may drag other stock markets down similarly, it is easy to see that a zero coupon bond yielding 6.3 percent meets the criterion of being a 50 percent better bargain. The bonds were a better bargain even if that relative status was due to a guarantee that the bond would not lose money if it was held until maturity.

Remember, the key to successful bargain hunting is to maintain a constant search for the best value in the financial markets. This search should be comprehensive enough to include all the stock markets around the world as well as the various bond markets. During extraordinary situations such as the height of the Internet bubble, that search can lead to the relative safety and fixed return of a bond. It is a matter of common sense. In 2000 you could stay invested in U.S. stocks that were likely to lose 50 percent of your money or buy government bonds that yielded 6.3 percent. That is an easy decision.

The decision to buy bonds at that point *could* have been based solely on a simple desire not to lose money. However, as true bargain hunters we must maintain an eye toward making money too. In this respect, the recommendation to purchase long-term government bonds was much more than a simple defensive measure. It was also an opportunity to make far more than the simple 6.3 percent yield offered on the 30-year zero coupon U.S. Treasury.

The reason for the added attractiveness of bonds was based on a long-standing relationship between the Federal Reserve Bank and its reaction to threats to the U.S. economy. In March 2000, the Internet bubble had reached such substantial highs and had persisted so long that it was affecting the consumption habits of American consumers. This is the same relationship we discussed in Chapter 6. The problem was that when the Internet bubble finally burst, a large percentage of American consumers who had been speculating in the stock market suddenly would feel much poorer. That could cause consumers to pull back on spending and possibly lead to an economic recession. In that event, Uncle John reasoned, the Federal Reserve would step in and take actions to lower interest rates that would bring relief to the economy by making money less expensive to obtain and use.

To provide some background on the Federal Reserve's role in this investment strategy, let us take a moment to highlight its possible actions. When you think about the role of the Federal Reserve in controlling interest rates, think about two actions it can take and the consequences of those actions. On the one hand, the Fed can lower interest rates; this is an *expansionary* policy because it stimulates demand for money as a result of the relative cheapness of money. An expansionary Fed policy is led by the Fed announcing a lower target for the federal funds rate at which depository institutions will make overnight loans between each other. This rate is targeted by the Federal Open Market Committee repurchasing treasuries in the market, which in turn replaces debt with more cash that can then be loaned. Think about it this way: If you were driving a car, these actions are equivalent to stepping on the accelerator.

On the other hand, the Fed can employ a *contractionary* policy. This would be implemented by selling Treasuries, which effectively would call in cash and replace it with debt to be paid back over time. In this case the Fed would be acting to raise interest rates to a targeted level, which makes money more expensive to obtain and use. If you are driving a car, these actions are akin to stepping on the brakes. The Fed typically uses an expansionary policy when the economy appears prone to recession or is in a recession and a contractionary policy when the economy is overheating and spurring inflation.

The Federal Reserve is composed of a chairman and a board of governors, who are all bright, well-heeled economists. They report to Congress and have no incentive to instigate or passively allow recessions. While recessions are a normal feature to any economy from time to time, the Fed will try to prevent them nonetheless. Therefore, they typically try to keep the economy out of recession as much as possible without risking a rise in inflation. Understanding that, Uncle John had a simple forecast for what would happen once the stock market bubble burst:

> Once the stock market bubble bursts, the Federal Reserve and the financial controllers in other nations will be in favor of lowering interest rates instead of raising interest rates. When interest rates go down, long-term bond prices go up.

Uncle John's view of what probably would unfold in the months and years to come had historical precedents. As with most events in the stock market, a careful bargain hunter usually can find a similar situation that occurred earlier. For that matter, within the history of stock market and economic events, finding a precedent for the Federal Reserve to lower interest rates and implement an expansionary policy in the face of a recession was relatively simple. More specifically, the Federal Reserve under Chairman Alan Greenspan's guidance had a strong tendency to react to shocks in the financial markets with interest rate cuts and an accommodative policy. In fact, the financial markets had become so accustomed to Greenspan cutting rates when the road got bumpy that financial market pundits coined the term the *Greenspan put*. That term refers to the idea that the markets will always get bailed out by an expansionary Fed policy. A put is a stock option that investors purchase to protect themselves from losses. Because this specific event was going to be driven largely by stock market excesses, insofar as it concerned consumer spending, it was reasonable to assume that the Federal Reserve would step in when the NASDAQ bubble finally popped.

Nevertheless, some believe that the Federal Reserve should react only to economic phenomena such as declining consumer spending, unemployment levels, and inflation levels. Yet others believe that the role of the Federal Reserve is to protect the overall financial system from shocks or problems. This would include problems that arise in the stock and bond markets. Greenspan had demonstrated a solid empirical tendency to employ the Federal Reserve's devices whenever there was a threat of a financial crisis such as a crash in the stock market.

Any bargain hunter requiring a historical precedent should look at two events in particular that bore a likeness to a looming crash in the NASDAQ. The first was the stock market crash of October 1987, and the second was the Russian debt default and the meltdown of the now-infamous hedge fund Long-Term Capital Management in 1998. In both instances the Federal Reserve reacted to a financial market crisis by easing interest rates and monetary policy. In the case of the building NASDAQ bubble and the potential fallout that could result, Uncle John felt comfortable with the likelihood that the Federal Reserve would act again to cut interest rates.

Now we can see clearly that bonds were not only a good way to protect our valuable money but also a likely way to make money if the Federal Reserve lowered interest rates. The Federal Reserve's willingness to protect the economy from recession would ensure that bonds would outpace most other investments in the few years after the crash of the Internet bubble. Simply put, as soon as the Federal Reserve began to lower interest rates, the prices of 30-year zero coupon Treasury bonds were set to rise substantially.

Perhaps even more interesting than Uncle John's forecast was the precision with which he prognosticated those events. He believed that around the time the NASDAQ fell 40 percent, long-term bonds would begin rising in price. Keep in mind that he made those judgments before any collapse or sign of weakness in the NASDAQ or the Internet bubble: *The time when people will be frightened and long-term bonds will begin to go up is when the major market indexes go down 40 percent. That will scare everyone, and many stocks will go down more. A lot will fall close to zero.*

By middle to late December of that year, the NASDAQ had fallen just over 40 percent from its March 15, 2000, high. Within another week, the Federal Reserve began cutting interest rates. The Fed started reducing rates on January 3, 2001, and continued to do so for the entire year (see Figure 9.1).

After reviewing the steady march downward in interest rates shown in Figure 9.1, bargain hunters should have an intuitive grasp of the accompanying rise in the price of zero coupon U.S. Treasury bonds. The rise in the price of that bond meant that holders of the bond were making money. In fact, witnessing such a deluge of interest rate cuts in one annual period should conjure up images of a ringing cash register for anyone long in zero coupon bonds. However, before we discuss the kinds of returns Uncle John was earning with this investment strategy, we need to take one more

Figure 9.1

Historical Changes to the Target Federal Funds Rate, 2001

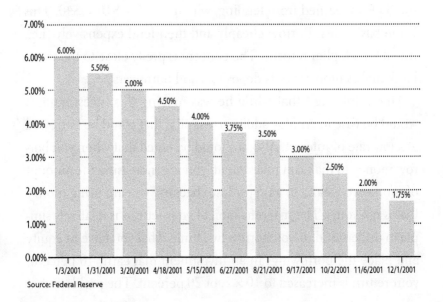

Source: Federal Reserve

step in our discussion. We start with a question: Do you think Uncle John was tying up his own cash in those risk-free bonds?

The answer is no. That introduces an investment strategy that some readers may have used, heard of, or encountered in the press. Uncle John was employing what often is called a *carry trade*. In its simplest form, a carry trade involves borrowing at a low rate of interest, say, 1 percent, and then lending the borrowed funds at a higher rate, perhaps 5 percent. As a borrower, you make payments at 1 percent but earn 5 percent on your investment. After you repay the borrowing cost, which is referred to as your *carry*, your profit is the difference between 1 percent and 5 percent, or 4 percent. To use a simple monetary example, let's say that you borrowed $1,000 and your cost to borrow is 1 percent interest on an annual basis, or $10 a year. You then take the borrowed $1,000 and lend it to a borrower who will pay you 5 percent on an annual basis, or $50 a year. After you pay the $10 you owe for interest, you can keep what is left of the $50 you earned from lending, which is $50 − $10 = $40. This is the basic idea: Borrow cheaply and then lend expensively (i.e., invest for a higher return). The concept is pretty close to the way a bank makes money on its depositors and borrowers.

Uncle John felt that while he was making this investment, it would be wise to employ additional capital that could be borrowed at a low rate of interest. Also, it should be noted that when you borrow money to make an investment, you are increasing the amount of money you stand to gain (or lose) because you are using money that is not yours. The magnification of your returns is relatively simple to understand: If you borrow two times what you have in equity and place the borrowings in an investment that earns 10 percent, your return is increased to 10 × 2, or 20 percent. The problem that investors run into is that the relationship also accelerates losses when an investment goes awry. If your investment using 2× leverage loses 10 percent, you actually have lost 10 × 2, or 20 percent. Leverage cuts both ways. The reason Uncle John was comfortable employing borrowed capital in this case was that he could secure a cost of borrowing that was exceedingly low and lend the capital to a borrower who had no risk of defaulting on the interest payments. In this case Uncle John turned to the lowest-cost funds in the world to borrow money for his carry trade: Japan.

Borrowing money in Japanese yen was by far the most attractive route because the effective interest rate at which Uncle John was borrowing yen at that time was 0.1 percent. Japan had exceedingly low interest rates because of the lasting effect of an economic downturn that was precipitated by its own stock market and real estate bubble. Japan had kept its interest rates at very low levels since its 1990 economic collapse in an effort to stimulate its economy back into meaningful growth.

Putting this together, if we were to take the borrowing rate of 0.1 percent in Japan and lend at a rate of 6.3 percent, we could lock in a rate of return of 6.2 percent, although we still run one important risk that could upset our returns. When we walk through the step-by-step process of what needs to be done to execute a carry trade, this risk becomes apparent. To begin, we borrow yen at a rate of 0.1 percent, take the yen, and convert them to U.S. dollars; with those U.S. dollars we purchase zero coupon 30-year Treasury strips denominated in U.S. dollars. However, if and when we sell the Treasury strips, we will need to take our U.S. dollar proceeds and convert them back into yen to repay the original loan. This creates a potential hazard. What if when we return to repay the loan, which is denominated in yen, the yen has appreciated in value against the U.S. dollar? Put another way, what if the U.S. dollar has lost value? The bottom line is that we are exposed to currency risk when we borrow in yen to buy something denominated in a different currency. This created a tangible risk in Uncle John's eyes because he saw the U.S. dollar as vulnerable to a major decline and has continued to believe it is vulnerable to declines in the years since.

To offset that risk, Uncle John shifted his focus from U.S. Treasury strips to zero coupon bonds representing other governments with more favorable currency dynamics. As we recall from our discussions of currency risks in earlier chapters, Uncle John always favored the currencies of countries that had positive trade balances; ran small budget deficits or, better yet, surpluses; and had small amounts of government borrowing relative to GDP. This list of criteria quickly made (and continues to make) the U.S. dollar relatively unattractive and vulnerable to decline. The United States fails on all these criteria primarily as a result of its large and increasing debt burden. However, there were other currencies available that had much more favorable dynamics than the dollar. Uncle John believed that Canada was a good alternative to the U.S. dollar and purchased long-term zero coupon bonds from that country instead. He also recommended zero coupon bonds from Australia and New Zealand. He believed that the currencies of those countries represented much safer plays than the U.S. dollar.

To provide some detail on what kinds of returns this investment generated, we can turn to the Canadian market for zero coupon bonds. Beginning in March 2000, around the time Uncle John made his recommendation to purchase those bonds, Canadian 30-year-maturity zero coupon bonds were yielding 5.3 percent. As interest rates fell over the years that followed as a result of general economic weakness, the investment produced a far larger return than the nominal 5.3 percent yield to maturity suggests.

For instance, if we take a three-year holding period, which is approximately how long it took for the U.S. indexes to bottom out in early 2003 from their long-standing bear market, the comparable yield on the bonds purchased in March 2000 fell to 4.9 percent from 5.3 percent. This may not sound like a big move, but as we walk through the returns, the returns add up quickly. For instance, when we calculate the return on the price of the zero coupon bonds in the market by applying these yields, the return in Canadian dollars was 31.9 percent. That 31.9 percent holding period return in Canadian dollars amounts to an annualized return of 9.7 percent, which is not bad for a risk-free return. However, if we take into account the weakness that Uncle John anticipated in the U.S. dollar and translate our returns from Canadian dollars to U.S. dollars, the return jumps to 43.4 percent, reaching 12.8 percent annualized, which also is not bad. As an aside, this means that the U.S. dollar lost 11.5 percent of its value during the holding period relative to the stronger Canadian currency.

Although these returns are impressive for an investment in a risk-free asset, we still are overlooking the effect of using borrowed money to purchase the bonds. When we take into account the use of 2× leverage, the holding period return translated back into U.S. dollars rises from 43.4 percent to 86.8 percent. In other words, using money that cost 0.1 percent to borrow, Uncle John invested in a risk-free zero coupon bond issued by the Canadian government and earned over 86 percent during a bear market that he anticipated would occur in the wake of the NASDAQ bust.

If we compare this 86 percent return with the performance of the NASDAQ index over the same period, we see that it *lost* 66 percent of its value from March 1, 2000, when Uncle John advised investors to purchase bonds. Uncle John's return on those bonds amounted to a compounded three-year annualized return of 25.5 percent.

The point of the discussion is that for a bargain hunter, it always pays to make relative comparisons. Sometimes the comparisons must extend into securities such as bonds. Although it represented an extreme situation in which Uncle John could not locate enough bargain stocks to place his money in, his process was sound enough to lead him into a profitable situation. His process is and always has been defined by commonsense decision making and a willingness to do things others do not. If we review his thought process on this trade, it came down to some simple questions: Should I risk losing substantial amounts of money in an inflated stock market or should I earn the 5 to 6 percent available in the various long-term bond markets? Anyone can see the logic behind this decision. The reasoning is simple, not complicated.

When he started purchasing the zero coupon bonds, Uncle John's plan was to hold the bonds up to the point where he could locate good stock bargains created by the bear market that would follow the bursting of the NASDAQ bubble: *If and when the NASDAQ index declines 50 percent, most investors may be wise to take a major part of their assets out of high-grade bonds to buy the shares that are the best bargains at that time.*

However, late in 2003 he changed his mind about investing in the United States primarily because he still saw all the major imbalances in the U.S. economy that led him to believe that the U.S.

dollar was vulnerable. Additionally, he spotted a new worrisome development. He believed that the United States was inflating a bubble with disastrous potential, except that bubble was not in the stock market. The bubble he saw inflating was in the U.S. housing market.

One of the key metrics he focuses on when valuing real estate is the replacement value of an asset. For example, just as he applied this method to the U.S. stock market at the time of the death of equities (see Chapter 5) he compares the market price with the cost of replacing a home. He said that he became alarmed when he noticed that buyers near his home in the Bahamas began paying four to five times the cost to construct a home. His concern was that prices would have to come back in line, and he had observed periods throughout history when prices were above the cost of reproduction as well as cycles in which prices of homes were below the cost of reproduction. Additionally, he said that prices had never been that far out of line with replacement costs in his lifetime. Although he did not think that a correction akin to the 90 percent declines witnessed during the Great Depression was possible, he did see the potential for a 50 percent decline. These comments that he made in the press may have left some observers with the feeling that there were no good opportunities for a bargain hunter to exploit. However, there was another investment to be made, and it will look very familiar now that we have discussed so many others over the course of his career. Next stop, China.

Chapter | 10

THE SLEEPING DRAGON
AWAKENS

*If a man takes no thought about what is distant, he
will find sorrow near at hand.*
—Confucius

In 1988, Uncle John appeared on the television show *Wall Street Week* with Louis Rukeyser, and one of the guests asked him what the next great investment opportunity in the world would be. His response included a brief rundown of previous great stock market investments by country. He mentioned that the United States had emerged as a great nation after World War I, and then Japan had followed after World War II. Then he paused for a moment and said that to him, China would be the next great nation and possibly a good investment. In his mind, the reunion of Hong Kong with China would provide that country with the strong and well-developed financial center it had been lacking and that progress would speed up tremendously. Years later, in a March 1990 interview for *Fortune* magazine, he summed up his view on the impact of Hong Kong rejoining China:

Hong Kong is rich in entrepreneurs who can start and run businesses, and there's a great shortage in mainland China of people who know how to do that. As a result, Hong Kong is likely to become the commercial and financial center for over a billion people, just as Manhattan is the commercial and financial center for a quarter of a billion people.

Today most readers and observers of financial markets take the significant economic presence of China in the world for granted. However, when Uncle John described China as the next great economic power in the world in 1988, nearly 20 years earlier, that was very forward thinking. Forward thinking is the calling card of successful bargain hunters.

If you consider the key attractions that lured Uncle John to Japan in the 1960s and South Korea in the late 1990s, you will see why he was drawn to China. To demonstrate, we will draw the key comparisons among the three countries: Japan, Korea, and China.

All three countries had hit rock bottom, and Uncle John believed they were certain to emerge from that period of despair. In the case of Japan, the country had been rendered economically prostrate by its disastrous fate in World War II. It was left in such a state of ruin that investors believed it would remain an irrelevant economic backwater going forward. In the same vein, when Japan began to rebuild, it attracted little serious attention from the major industrial nations, including the United States and Europe. The industrial nations saw no impending threat from Japan, a producer of "cheap trinkets" in the 1950s.

South Korea was a nation left in economic devastation by the destruction caused by the Korean War. Much like Japan before it, South Korea relied heavily on the financial aid of developed nations as it went through a rebuilding process during the 1960s. When it took aim at becoming an industrial power, few believed there was any such capability in a country whose third largest export at that time was human hair wigs.

In the case of China, no historical headline war event sent the country into an economic tailspin. With a slightly closer look, though, we can see that political events within China during the middle to late twentieth century dismantled its economy and left the nation in shambles. More specifically, we are referring to the regime of the communist leader Mao Tse-Tung and his implementation of first the Great Leap Forward and then the Cultural Revolution. Both of those events left the country with the results that would have followed from losing a major war.

The Great Leap Forward was an economic strategy developed and implemented by Mao in 1958 to move the country toward joint industrial and agrarian progress. A central tenet of that strategy was that the state could manage the agricultural process, which then would generate the funds necessary for industrial ventures into steel production and eventually more advanced goods. The first move by Mao to install the program involved the widespread collectivization of farmland into communes (which had been used earlier on a much smaller scale). This essentially meant that all property ownership was abolished, and reports suggest that 700 million Chinese were relocated into farming communes, with about 5,000 families per commune. Once the families were relocated, they were forced to work in the fields to produce food for the country and fund the industrialization process.

Most bargain hunters will recall from earlier chapters that when the government nationalizes or expropriates private property, whether land or a business, that stifles productivity and kills the spirit of progress. Countries that implement those strategies make horrible investments as the effects are manifested in the economy. In the case of China, the initial steps set the country on a fast track in the wrong direction. Partly because of Mao's willingness to lock up or expunge anyone who spoke against his policies and partly because of his stubbornness in not admitting a mistake sooner, the end result was massive starvation and loss of life.

Matters worsened when Mao attempted to install his simultaneous project of industrialization alongside the collectivization of the agricultural economy. Having been convinced by a provincial government official that small-scale "backyard" steel furnaces were the most appropriate way to develop the steel industry, Mao directed every commune and urban neighborhood to install and use a backyard furnace for steel production.

Mao probably was encouraged enough by the reports of excess farming production in the communes that he thought it was time to put the Great Leap Forward into high gear. The truth was that the production of the communes was woefully insufficient. The people forced into farming had little incentive to produce except fear of retribution. Regardless of their spirits, they were using poor farming techniques and poorer tools constructed hastily and without quality controls in China's factories. To compound matters, local government officials inflated the communes' production statistics. Those lies probably were driven by the hopes of central government approbation or fear of the threat of retribution for not meeting set goals. Either way, the statistics were inflated and inflated again to show communes exceeding their goals.

Supporters of the Great Leap in the central government took that information as a signal to continue exporting food, believing there was a surplus, as well as pull workers out of the fields to dedicate more resources to the backyard furnace steel industry. Anyone in the central government who knew the true conditions dared not speak up and draw criticism. All told, the growing shortages of food were accelerated by those central government actions, and before long people in the communes were starving.

By 1960 grain production had fallen 15 percent from the inadequate level in 1959. The backyard steel furnaces also proved to be a total disaster as the products that resulted from melting scrap in the poorly run furnaces were too weak to be used for building. The absence of proper fuel for the furnaces led workers to remove doors from houses to burn to keep the furnaces operating. In sum, the Great Leap Forward was a complete economic failure that produced severe humanitarian consequences. By the time Mao succumbed to the unavoidable reality of widespread famine in 1960 and lowered his profile to avoid taking responsibility for those errors, a range of estimates from different sources suggests that 30 million people may have died.

Mao conceded visible power to the prominent officials Liu Shaoqi and Deng Xiaopeng because of the debacle and became chairman of the Communist Party. Before long he regretted fading quietly into the background. In 1966, Mao set the wheels in motion to regain his lost influence by instigating the Cultural Revolution. The Cultural Revolution was a political maneuver instigated by Mao to oust his competition in the government. Mao did this because the new leadership had gained popularity and appeal by reversing his reforms from the Great Leap Forward.

The Cultural Revolution once again put China in a state of crisis. One devastating by-product was Mao's support of the Red

Guards, who began as a group of students defending Maoism and intent on defeating the "old ways" of the "bourgeoisie." Mao embraced the movement since he viewed it as a vehicle to create sweeping change and an unbridled acceptance of socialism throughout China. Part of that process was the eradication of "the four olds": old customs, old culture, old habits, and old ideas. The Red Guards had unlimited authority to enforce this dismissal of the four olds, and since they numbered in the millions, they exercised it ruthlessly. The army and police were instructed to stand down and not interfere with the Red Guards' actions or they would be considered to be defending the bourgeoisie and prosecuted.

The Red Guards took the opportunity to destroy churches, ancient buildings, antiques, books, and paintings and to torture and kill innocent people. Some estimates put the casualties from the Cultural Revolution at 500,000 people or more. By 1968, the Red Guards had grown to such a substantial size that Mao felt they were threatening the central government's authority and ordered them disbanded. The Cultural Revolution's spirit of radical bullying persisted until the "gang of four" was arrested in 1976. The gang was a group of powerful and high-ranking instigators (including Mao's estranged wife) who were central to the drive of the Cultural Revolution under Mao.

As terrible as this event sounds from a humanitarian perspective, its consequences were equally severe and lasting on China's economy. During the Cultural Revolution nearly all economic activity shut down as the populace became concerned primarily with persecuting the old ways or running from persecution. The government's financial resources were redirected to support the Red Guard, and anyone who qualified as an "intellectual" was sent to a work camp for reeducation, including the two leaders Mao purged. College entrance exams were canceled, and education stalled. The lost 10 years in the educational system produced a gaping hole in China's progress.

Only in 1977, after Deng Xiaopeng reemerged from a work camp to lead China again, did the country reinstitute its education system and implement serious reforms to undo the substantial damage caused by Mao over the previous two decades. Although not an official head of state, Deng Xiaopeng had something of a day-to-day CEO role for China after he returned in 1974 at the request of the ailing premier and with permission from Mao. Soon after the premier's death in 1976, Deng was purged again by the gang of four, but after their arrest he was able to regain traction in the political system and reemerge as Mao's de facto successor after Mao's death.

With Deng in control in 1977, China instituted a complete reversal and an open repudiation of the Cultural Revolution. Deng's intention to elevate the Chinese from their despair was made clear in 1979, when he said that "to get rich is glorious." Deng's emphasis was on the notion that "socialism does not mean shared poverty." His road to rebuilding China from its economic ruin was hardly a sure thing, though. One major obstacle was the "Down to the Countryside Movement" of 1968, in which Mao ordered all "intellectuals" to move from the cities to the country. Those intellectuals included children recently out of grade school. Deng was facing the prospect of an entirely lost generation in a society with deep scars from the Cultural Revolution. His strategy to rebuild China needed to be successful, and he desired precedent and careful thought, which was in stark contrast to Mao's approach. Not surprisingly, Deng began to open China's market to the West, though slowly and cautiously. He had found a successful economic model to pattern China's growth on in an old Chinese neighbor: Japan.

As you may recall from our earlier discussions of Japan and South Korea, there is a basic recipe that each of those Asian countries applied to rebuild its economy rapidly. The Chinese were attracted to that recipe and began implementing it in their own way. In each instance, a heavy savings rate is a major prerequisite for economic success. A high savings rate is an attribute that Uncle John often favors in making foreign investments. China proved adept at creating a large rate of saving across the country. In fact, by the time Uncle John had mentioned China as the next great nation for investment in 1988, the country had achieved one of the highest savings rates in the world alongside Korea and Japan (see Figure 10.1).

Figure 10.1

Gross National Savings Percentage of GDP for China, South Korea, and Japan

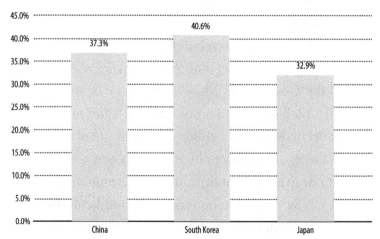

Sources: OECD, Asian Development Bank

Figure 10.2

Balance of Trade in China (Exports-Imports Percentage of GDP)

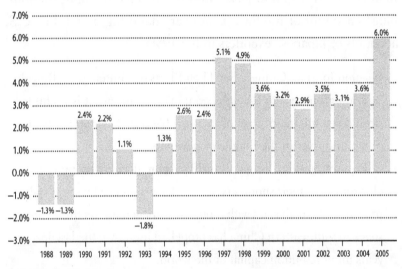

Source: Asian Development Bank

This heavy savings rate was the same strategy used by Japan and Korea to build financial reserves and finance industrial growth. That growth would drive increasing exports with more value-added content over time. China was determined to have the same success in exports that Japan and Korea had experienced in their rebuilding processes. Like them, China began at the low end of the market by manufacturing textiles and "cheap stuff" for export. That concentration on exports most often produced a trade surplus, which is another economic condition that Uncle John likes to find in a country. Figure 10.2 shows the relationship between exports and imports over time as a percentage of China's GDP.

Chinese exports grew rapidly over time, but at the outset (like Japan's trinkets and Korea's wigs) the goods were decidedly at the low end. In the following excerpt from the *New York Times* published in

1993, a reporter covers an export-driven town in southern China. Qiaotou became known as the button capital of the world; that is, it manufactured shirt and jacket buttons. Not surprisingly, the journalist's account of the town is not very flattering, much like U.S. accounts of Japanese exporters in the 1950s.

> Qiaotou Journal; Chinese Bet Their Shirts on Buttons and, Bingo!
>
> For a glimpse into China's economic revolution, it is useful to stroll down the main street of this humble little town on the banks of a putrid river in the middle of nowhere.
>
> Peasants amble along the dusty pavement, carrying protesting chickens over their shoulders, as rickshaws squeeze by street stalls pressing in on both sides with mounds of bric-a-brac. Yet this remote speck in southeastern China has propelled itself over the last dozen years into the button capital of the world.
>
> Each year, the privately run factories of Qiaotou produce about 12 billion buttons, overwhelmingly the humdrum plastic kind found on cheap shirts and jackets. This button boom, amounting to two buttons annually per inhabitant on earth, has transformed rice paddies into factory districts, and peasants into tycoons.

Pay careful attention to the ambition of the button manufacturers. Like the Japanese and Koreans before them, those manufacturers were not content making just buttons; they were ready to move up the ladder into higher-value products, even if those products were just tennis shoes. In the following excerpt from the same article, the reporter interviews one of the button manufacturers in Qiaotou, who captures the spirit of those budding industrialists.

> "I'm planning to start more factories and maybe start exporting," Mr. Zhan said, shaking his 24-karat gold bracelet, one so huge that

it could double as an arm weight for working out. He was sitting on a leather couch in the living room of his new six-story home; he cannot figure out what to do with all the space, so the top three floors are empty.

"I may diversify into manufacturing of tennis shoes," Mr. Zhan added thoughtfully.

"Who knows what it'll be like in 10 years? But the bigger, the better!"

The article does a good job of fleshing out the situation in China. China was falling in love with capitalism and, of course, the spoils that follow business success. The people needed little more than Deng's prompt to strike while the iron was hot.

Perhaps more important than the ambition of the Chinese was their ability to execute their strategy. If we take a look at the country's exports and their composition over time, we can see the familiar progression from a onetime exporter of low-grade textiles mature to an exporter of industrial machinery and higher-value-added products. If we compare the percentage of exports accounted for by textiles in 1992 with the percentage in 2005, we see a dramatic reversal. That reversal was accompanied by tremendous growth and a higher percentage of exports in machinery, mechanical appliances, and electrical equipment. In sum, textiles shrank to half their original percentage from 1992 and machinery increased to a percentage that was three times the 1992 level. This reversal from low-valued-added goods to more sophisticated exports of industrial goods mirrors the earlier advances in Japan and Korea (see Figure 10.3).

China's combination of high savings and investment in its industrial base, along with the exports that resulted, propelled the economy into a growth rate envied by most nations. In the same manner as

Figure 10.3

The Shift in Chinese Exports from Textiles to Machinery, 1992–2005

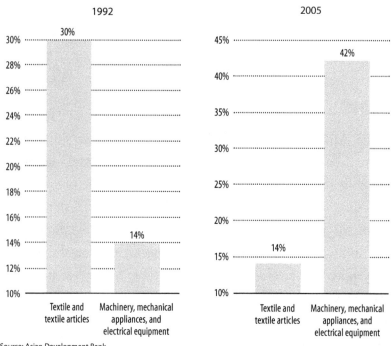

Source: Asian Development Bank

Japan and Korea before it, China has posted the leading growth rate in the world during its economic transformation (see Figure 10.4).

China's growth rate has been impressive, and Uncle John believes that it has put China on track to overtake the United States and have the largest economy in the world in the next 30 years. China's success thus far in transforming its economy from a socialist system to a free market system has been fairly well recognized. Despite these positives, though, China remains a work in progress. One of the areas still in progress is its restrictions on foreign investment.

Figure 10.4

Top Average Growth Rates in Annual GDP, 1980–2005

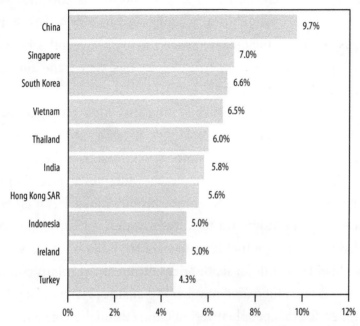

Source: IMF

Foreign investors still have a difficult time accessing shares on the local markets of mainland China: the Shanghai and Shenzhen exchanges. However, there are Chinese American Depositary Receipts (ADRs) trading in the U.S. market. There are also many Chinese companies listed on the exchanges of Hong Kong and Singapore that foreign investors can access easily. China traditionally has been wary of foreign investment, partly as a result of foreign occupation and colonization over the course of its history. Furthermore, the Chinese are deeply proud and nationalistic. On one occasion when we discussed China with Uncle John, he remarked, "The thing to always remember about China has to do with the people. . . . You must not think of them as communists or capitalists. . . . They are Chinese first, and that is how they see themselves." This nationalism, accompanied by outside investors' cautiousness about the opaqueness of the market, reports of occasional corruption, and the risk of loss, has kept some foreign investors away over the years.

Uncle John's approach to investing in China has remained opportunistic and selective. Sticking to his bargain hunter discipline, he has made some investments in China over the last several years. However, in the absence of a widespread correction in that market, he has been selective in his purchases. His methods for investing in China also have been varied. In early 2003 he invested in various mutual fund devices focused on China when the worldwide decline in share prices during the previous couple of years led to an increased number of bargains. He generally has recommended that people invest in China through managers who have their "feet on the ground," which helps lower the risk of investing in a relatively opaque market. In other words, he thinks it is prudent to invest with managers who are using local analysts who are able to visit the companies and keep up on local information. This helps safeguard against corruption and other managerial risks. At the same time, Uncle John has invested in individual stocks when he has found good bargains. Two stocks that Uncle John found attractive in China in September 2004 were China Life Insurance and China Mobile.

China Life Insurance is the largest life insurance company operating in China, and in 2004 its stock became attractive to Uncle John for a number of reasons. Primarily, he saw the stock as a vehicle to access the strength of the Chinese currency without paying a premium. Because the stock is traded as an ADR on the New York Stock Exchange, he could purchase a highly liquid security without paying the high fees otherwise necessary to purchase Chinese Renminbi. At the same time, he could gain access to the underlying investments that China Life was making. Uncle John reasoned that insurers investing the premiums paid to them by customers always seek to protect themselves from currency fluctuations, and so they are likely to match the currencies they invest in with the currencies with which they transact business. This lowers the risk that currency movements will disrupt their ability to do business when they pay out claims. Therefore, by purchasing shares of the insurer he was also accessing the local Chinese currency, which he found attractive over the long-term. China Life seemed like a good bargain: Uncle John feared a decline in value of the U.S. dollar, and the Chinese economy had several attractive features that often lead to a strong currency. Also, this was a growing business with a relatively attractive valuation.

Uncle John's strategy with China Life is similar to a strategy he routinely employed when investing in emerging markets. Throughout Uncle John's career he found foreign stock markets that were attractive bargains but were perhaps too small for him to make a substantial investment. One method he applied to compensate for the lack of liquidity in those situations was to purchase the stocks of large banks operating in those countries. Banks operating in an emerging market country often invest in that country's stock market. In many cases, the banks already owned the stocks that Uncle John found attractive. When the stocks owned by the banks increased in value, the banks also would increase in value. This method of accessing stocks in markets with liquidity issues had been successful for Uncle John in the past.

China Life had a similar dynamic; however, in this case he was more concerned with being invested in a currency that over the long term had much better underlying fundamentals than the U.S. dollar. Uncle John has always used the technique of examining the true values of assets on company's balance sheets. He is an expert at exploiting hidden values such as the undisclosed unconsolidated subsidiaries of listed Japanese companies in the 1960s and the often overlooked security holdings of banks in emerging markets. It always pays to dig into the financial statements and look for not so obvious values that create a bargain. This relationship, coupled with the attractiveness of a long-term growing business in a developing market, led Uncle John to purchase shares of China Life Insurance in 2004.

We have learned a great deal from Uncle John over the years. One of the most important lessons is to buy his stock recommendations. Simply put, if he recommends a stock, buy it! As you can see in Figure 10.5, we are particularly grateful for the return on our investment in China Life: approximately 1,000 percent in three years.

We now take a look at Uncle John's other purchase and recommendation: China Mobile, is a cellular telecommunication company. The company currently leads the Chinese market, having captured nearly 68 percent of its customer base. Although China Mobile costs a good deal more than it did back in 2004, it still provides a good historical example of some of Uncle John's preferred criteria in a stock. This stock also trades as an ADR on the New York Stock Exchange. First, the stock had a relatively low P/E ratio of 11x. More important, the P/E ratio looked even better when

Figure 10.5

China Life Insurance ADR—Three-Year Return Since September 2004

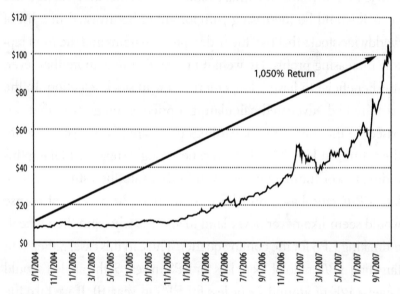

Source: Bloomberg

coupled with the long-term estimated growth rate in earnings per share of approximately 20 percent. Taking this a step further, the P/E divided by the estimated long-term growth rate for earnings per share (PEG ratio) of 0.55 (P/E of 11× divided by an estimated growth rate of 20) made it one of the lowest-priced stocks in the world in the wireless telecommunications industry. In other words, this stock was among the cheapest in the world compared with the remaining list of global wireless telecommunication companies:

- China Mobile 2004 PEG ratio = 0.55
- Worldwide wireless telecommunication 2004 group average PEG ratio = 0.84

Perhaps most important to Uncle John was the company's strong growth rate and high earning power on a comparative basis. When Uncle John invested in China Mobile, he said that over the next five years it would be increasingly important to be invested in a list of worldwide stocks that had the widest profit margins and the most rapidly increasing profits. He went on to say that now more than ever, it is beneficial to have a longer-term view in stock selection. In the past, he had advocated calculating a price/earnings ratio that was based on the estimation of earnings per share (EPS) five years into the future. In late 2004, however, he strongly suggested taking this estimation of future earnings even further into the future to calculate a P/E ratio based on EPS in year 10, or 2015. This of course would seem like never-never land to analysts who spin their wheels estimating EPS for the coming quarter. Thus, in this case, rather than targeting a P/E ratio of 5× or less for EPS in year 5, the analyst should target a P/E of around 2× or less for EPS in year 10. If we take the same set of assumptions that we applied to China Mobile in 2004 (a P/E based on the current year's EPS of 11× and the assumption of a long-term growth rate in EPS of 20 percent) and extend those relationships out into time, we arrive at a calculated P/E ratio of 1.8× year 10 EPS (current price in 2004 divided by estimated EPS in year 10). Looking at a stock with this long-term perspective is challenging, but the results can be rewarding (see Figure 10.6).

Uncle John was the first to admit that the task of estimating what a company's EPS will be 10 years into the future is very difficult. If one places a heavy emphasis on the companies with the best growth and strongest earnings power, it is easy to see where this exercise directs a bargain hunter. As in attempting to calculate the EPS of a company five years into the future, the bargain hunter is forced to take a long-term perspective on the company. Not even a minute

Figure 10.6

China Mobile ADR—Three-Year Return Since September 2004

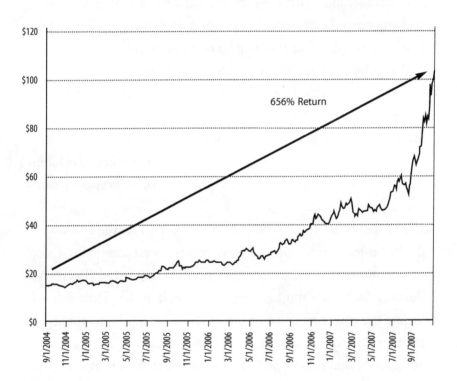

656% Return

Source: Bloomberg

should be wasted thinking about something like the next quarter's EPS. Instead, Uncle John's advice to forecast EPS 10 years down the road provides a strong warning about the growing threat of building surpluses in the economy and the resulting future competition that excess capacities will impose on profit margins and earnings.

Therefore, by focusing on the future prospects of a company as much as 10 years into the future, a bargain hunter has to think about the competitive positioning of a company in the market. In short, bargain hunters must devote a large majority of their efforts to determining the competitive advantage of a business in relation to its competitors. This requires putting a great deal of effort into studying not only the company whose stock you are considering for purchase but also that company's competitors in the market.

Uncle John always said that when he visited a company in his early days as an analyst, he always got the best information from the company's competitors, not from the company itself. The aim of this analysis is to get a sense of how well a company will be able to maintain its profitability into the future. This is a key consideration if you are going to make an estimation of a company's earnings 10 years ahead.

The key factor that all bargain hunters must consider is one of the first rules in economics: Excess profits attract competition, and competition will build until excess profits are squeezed. Therefore, the bargain hunter must ask questions such as this: How defensible are the company's profit margins in the face of increasing competition? It is an encouraging sign if the company has competitive advantages that other competitors cannot replicate. Perhaps the company is the low-cost producer or has a superior image in the market, with its brands preferred by the majority of customers. If the company has a large percentage of market share, with the remaining market share divided among a few companies that have no interest in waging a price war, that too can be a good sign. The key question is, How easy would it be for someone else to replicate this business? If it is very easy to replicate, it is more probable that competition will affect the profit margins and growth rate of the company. Conversely, if it is very difficult to replicate, the earnings stream may be considered more valuable to an investor.

In mid-2005, Uncle John shared his thoughts on the growing levels of competition among businesses as well as nonprofits such as universities. His discussion was couched in the context of his concern over the rising levels of U.S. debt and the impending collapse of the U.S. housing bubble:

> Accelerating competition is likely to cause profit margins to continue to decrease and even become negative in various industries. Over ten-fold more persons, hopelessly indebted, leads to multiplying bankruptcies; not only for them, but for many businesses that extend credit without collateral. When this occurs, voters are likely to insist on rescue-type subsidies, which transfer the debts to governments, such as Fannie Mae and Freddie Mac. Research and discoveries in efficiency are likely to continue to accelerate.
>
> Not yet have I found any better method to prosper . . . than to keep your net worth in shares in those corporations which have proven to have the widest profit margins and the most rapidly increasing profits. Earning power is likely to continue to be valuable, especially if diversified among many nations.

These views express concern about the conditions of the economy, in particular the housing bubble, in the United States. Uncle John's examination of the debt levels of the U.S. consumer and the large rise in home prices far above the cost of reproduction led him to take a cautious position on the stock market and have a preference for companies with the best mix of high growth and large profit margins over the coming years. What perhaps is more important than his views on the housing bubble and the increasing value of high-quality growing earnings streams is his noticeable willingness to continue innovating, even at the age of 93, when he made these investment recommendations. If there is one thing that all investors and bargain hunters alike can take away from Uncle John, it is his consistent effort to look at matters from a different perspective. When he sensed that more investors were concentrating on near-term earnings trends in companies, he advocated looking even farther out into the future prospects of a company. Five years would be okay, but 10 years would be even better.

As we tie all this back into our discussion of his investments in China, we can see another important point. As much as Uncle John admires China and its rapid progress, he remains a highly disciplined bargain hunter. His approach is to invest only when he spots a bargain, not under any other circumstance.

Always looking for investments differently than others do (whether in a different country, with a different method, with a different time horizon, with a different level of optimism, or with a different level of pessimism) is the only way to separate yourself from the crowd. By now you should know that the only way to achieve superior investment results is to buy what others are despondently selling and sell what others are avidly buying in the market.

> *If you want to have a better performance than the crowd,*
> *you must do things differently from the crowd.*
> —Sir John Templeton

AFTERWORD

We hope that you enjoyed reading our book. It gave us great pleasure to review and describe a sampling of Sir John Templeton's wise investments from his many decades as a successful bargain hunter. At the same time, we understand that while all our readers may possess a bit of the bargain hunter in them, it remains a tremendous undertaking both from a time and a skill standpoint to successfully purchase individual stocks for one's own brokerage account. The truth is, it is a full-time job. Likewise, some readers may possess the spirit of the bargain hunter without engaging any interest in the study of subjects such as finance, accounting, or economics. For this reason, we have offered a brief list of professional bargain hunters who have displayed similar wisdom and comparable methods to Sir John in the management of their mutual funds. You may choose to investigate these managers, or blaze a path of your own. In any event we feel relatively safe listing these managers, since your authors, as well as Sir John Templeton himself, have invested with them from time to time over the years. We receive no compensation or benefit from listing these managers, but remember that you should always investigate for yourself. Happy bargain hunting.

Dodge & Cox Funds
Franklin Templeton Investments
Friess Associates, Inc.
Matthews International Capital Management, LLC·
Royce & Associates, Inc.
Southeastern Asset Management, Inc.
Third Avenue Management, LLC
Tweedy, Browne Company, LLC

INDEX

John M. Templeton's
father, Harvey Maxwell
Templeton Sr.
(1876–1960).

Harvey Maxwell
Templeton Sr.

John M. Templeton's mother, Vella Handly Templeton in Winchester, Tennessee, 1907.

John M. Templeton with elder brother Harvey M. Templeton Jr. in Winchester, Tennessee, ca. 1916.

John M. Templeton with elder brother, Harvey Maxwell Templeton Jr.

John M. Templeton with his mother, Vella Handly Templeton

John M. Templeton (front row, third from left) at Central High School, Winchester, Tennessee.

John Marks Templeton Sr. aboard ship in 1934 en route to England to take the Rhodes scholarship.

John Marks Templeton Sr. with Judith D. Folk in New York, 1934.
Couple married on April 17, 1937.

John M. Templeton with his three children (left to right):   John M.
Templeton Jr., Christopher Templeton, John M. Templeton Sr., and
daughter, Anne Templeton—Christmas 1956.

Rome, 1958. Left to Right: Christopher Templeton, Malcolm Butler, Irene Templeton, Anne Templeton, Wendy Butler, John M. Templeton Sr., Harvey M. Templeton III, Jill Templeton, John M. Templeton, Jr., and Handly C. Templeton.

John M. Templeton Sr. with Louis Rukeyser.

Her Majesty Queen Elizabeth II greets Sir John M. Templeton.

Sir John Templeton at the exact North Pole, July 27, 1996, keeps abreast of financial affairs with a slightly out-of-date *Wall Street Journal*.

John M. Templeton Foundation, Annual Members' Meeting, Nassau, Bahamas, 2005.